Greenpatch Book

You Animal!

Written by Jerry Booth
Illustrated by Nancy King

Who Is a Greenpatch Kid?

Anyone. Maybe you. All over the world, young people who care about the earth are doing things: helping to save habitats; protecting endangered animals; helping to clean up pollution. If *you* believe that humans need to take better care of the earth, and if you are ready to do your part, you may already be a Greenpatch Kid. For more information about the kids' environmental movement and how you can participate, see page 48.

A Gulliver Green Book
Harcourt Brace & Company
San Diego New York London

Library of Congress Cataloging-in-Publication Data is available on request. ISBN 0-15-200696-6

First edition A B C D E

Gulliver Green® Books focus on various aspects of ecology and the environment, and a portion of the proceeds from the sale of these books will be donated to protect, preserve, and restore native forests. *A Greenpatch Book* is a registered trademark of Harcourt Brace & Company.

This book is dedicated
to Greenpatch Kids everywhere.

Printed in Singapore

Some of the Things in This Book

Greenpatch Kids: Real kids doing real things.
See pages 7, 11, 31, 37, 44.
Where can I find a list of all the animals and projects in this book?
See the index on page 47.
What does that weird word mean?
See the glossary on page 46.
Where can I go to learn more?
See the resources section on page 45.
I want to be a Greenpatch Kid. What do I do?
See the Greenpatch box on page 48.

Can You Name This Animal?

It can only live on a third of Earth's surface because it lacks gills for obtaining oxygen from water. Unlike turtles, its breathing seems limited to two openings in its head. It loses its tail before birth, so it's not very good in trees. Though it moves on land and water, it's rather slow on both. It has poor eyesight. A hawk can see eight times as far. Its vision is limited to a small sliver of the light spectrum. It can't see the landing patterns that bees use for locating pollen-bearing flowers or the heat patterns that snakes use to locate prey. Though it's constantly making sounds with its flexible tongue, it's practically deaf. Its hearing is so limited it can't hear two-thirds of the things that elephants say. It definitely doesn't eat much grass. Grazing animals have strong second stomachs for breaking down food. This animal only has a tiny appendix where its second stomach used to be. Its muscles are puny and no match for the smaller chimpanzee. A swat from an elephant's trunk would easily crush its fragile skeleton. Its most curious feature is the large dome that teeters on the top of its backbone. The brain inside this dome isn't as big as a whale's or an elephant's, but it's very large for such a small creature. The adult animals care for the young for 15 to 25 years, longer than many animals' entire lives! It seems to have a high sense of self-importance. It gave

itself a name that indicates it believes itself to be the only animal capable of thinking. It likes to be around others of its kind. Sometimes you find thousands of them crowded together. At other times, it will destroy thousands of its own kind for no apparent reason. Who is this odd but interesting animal? *Homo sapiens*, naturally. That's you, you animal!

Animals Can

You're a remarkable animal. But don't get too smug. There are a lot of other remarkable creatures, too!

An amoeba has only one cell, but it can do many of the things you can do—capture and digest food, eliminate wastes, and avoid danger. But when it's time to reproduce, it acts more like a plant! Can you do that?

Elephants can talk with one another miles apart, using sounds we can't even hear. Try doing that without a telephone!

A turtle's spine and skin have evolved into an architectural wonder that combines strength and lightness. How does your spine protect your body?

Chameleons can make their moods perfectly clear without saying a word. And they can move each eye independently of the other. Try doing that!

The shape of an owl's face helps it see in the dark.

A mole can dig almost as fast as you can walk.

Chimps can run faster on their knuckles than the fastest human sprinters.

Putting Us Where We Belong

Did you guess that we were describing humans? Probably. That's because you share one of the most remarkable human features—a big brain. This single feature alone makes up for all our other "weaknesses." Without it we'd have become extinct long ago.

Think about it for a minute. Our brains have helped us survive, even though we're not as big, fast, strong, or observant as other animals. Even with a big brain, we're still animals.

Every animal is powerful in its own way. You have a large brain, whereas a cheetah has a specialized skeleton for running at fast speeds. You have opposable thumbs for grasping objects, whereas a turtle has a protective shell. Your upright posture frees your hands for holding objects; a giraffe's posture

allows it to feed in the tallest trees. Each adaptation helps an animal survive and thrive.

Human actions have got the world into a lot of trouble—we've cut down forests, polluted rivers, fouled the air, and destroyed other animals' habitats. It's about time we began using our big brains to solve some of these problems. The first step is to realize that we're not better or more important than other animals. Just different.

We're the dominant animal right now, but dominance is fleeting. Think about the dinosaurs. Did you know that at one time these large reptiles were the dominant species on Earth? They're all gone.

Humans are interesting animals. So next time you want to study a curious species, don't visit the zoo, check out the mall. Once you know what to look for, you'll begin to see the animal in all of us.

Compared to You

Think about all the animal comparisons humans make. A muscular person is "strong as an ox." A clever person is "smart as a fox." When you're really angry, someone might say you're "mad as a wet hen."

Snake in the grass. Crazy like a fox. A wise old owl. Eats like a bird. Crocodile tears. Dead as a dinosaur. What do humans mean by all these animal similes?

Try to think of other animal comparisons we use. Then take it one step further. Pretend you're an animal. What human comparisons would you make? If you were a cheetah, it might be "slow as a human." But what if you were a hawk? What other animals would make interesting comparisons?

Make a list of animal comparisons that humans use. How many of them are positive? How many are negative? Does this tell you anything about how humans think about other animals?

Deep in the forest, the rains fell steadily throughout the winter. Large puddles of muddy water flooded the low spots on the forest floor. Millions of microscopic creatures came to life in the dark brown waters. Among them, the amoebae (A MEE BEE) hunted and foraged through their nutrient-rich environment. With the first days of spring, however, sunlight returned to the forest floor. Day by day, the puddles began to shrink. Though their world was slowly disappearing, the amoebae didn't disappear. Instead, they came together in ever larger groups. By the time the last drops of the puddle disappeared early that summer, there, in the mud amongst the damp leaves, was an inch-wide yellow blob. The amoebae had formed a slime mold.

The small blob oozed slowly through the leaves, grazing on the debris, meeting and merging with other slime molds. Soon it was four inches wide. By late summer it had doubled again. But soon the ground dried to a fine dust. The slime mold oozed onto a nearby log and stopped moving. It began to change again. Small domes appeared on its surface. On a breezy afternoon, these domes burst, throwing thousands of spores up into the air. A soft breeze carried the spores through the forest. With the first autumn rains, they will come to life and begin the cycle again.

It Comes from the Muck!
It's Neither Plant nor Animal!

Slime molds are a life form you probably don't notice too often. Yet once you get down on your knees, put your nose to the ground, and start looking for them, you can find them almost everywhere—oozing along through damp leaves or clinging to the sides of rotten logs.

Mycologists—scientists who study fungi and other related creatures—think slime molds are fascinating. A slime mold really lives three lives: first, as a microscopic amoeba, then as a blob-shaped grazer that can grow as big as your hand, and finally as a spore-producing formation that acts a lot like a plant.

At different points in its life, a slime mold acts like an animal and a plant, but it's neither. Scientists put slime molds in a group called Protista. This group includes everything from 100-foot-tall giant kelp to *Giardia* (JAR DEE AH), a microscopic organism that lives in water and can give humans severe stomach pains if they swallow it. In some ways, Protista is like the "junk drawer" of biology. It's where scientists put all the life forms that don't fit anywhere else.

The Shapeless Wonder

What shape is your body? What gives it that shape? Skin, bones, muscles? Now imagine that your body didn't have a fixed shape. Where would your front be? How about your back? Even up and down might get sort of confusing. Think about how different your life would be if your body could assume any shape it wanted.

An amoeba is a microscopic creature that doesn't have a fixed shape. Its body can take on any shape. In fact, that's how it moves. It simply shoots part of its body out in the direction it wants to go. These fingerlike growths are called *pseudopods* (SOOD O PODS), or "false feet." Once a pseudopod is extended, the rest of the fluid inside the amoeba's cell, its *cytoplasm* (SITE O PLAZ UM), simply flows into it. Pretty soon the amoeba isn't where it used to be.

Turning on a Dime

When an amoeba wants to change directions, it doesn't have to turn around. After all, it doesn't have a front or a back, so how could it turn? It simply shoots a pseudopod out in the new direction and flows into it. Having a shapeless body makes things a lot easier. Think about all the contortions you go through to change directions: your brain thinks about turning, your eyes scan for obstacles and give the OK, and your brain sends new directions to your muscles, which in turn move your skeleton. Life would be a lot simpler if we could simply reshape our bodies. Life's tough for us complex animals!

Ooze Engulfs Prey! Then Dissolves It!

An amoeba not only moves by reshaping its body, that's how it hunts and feeds, too. Amoebae eat other creatures just as humans do, so they must constantly track down and trap microscopic food that is even smaller than themselves.

We're not sure how an amoeba locates its prey, but when it does, it oozes right up and extends its pseudopods out and around the prey's body. Sometimes the amoeba even sends a pseudopod over the top of the prey to prevent an escape. Once the amoeba has completely surrounded the prey, it begins to slowly dissolve it away . . . sort of like you do when you suck on a jawbreaker!

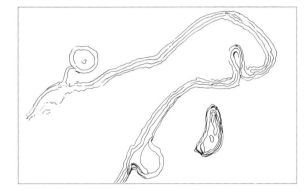

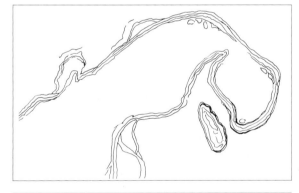

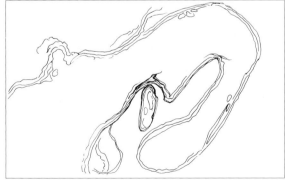

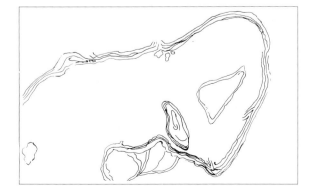

Amoeba Watching

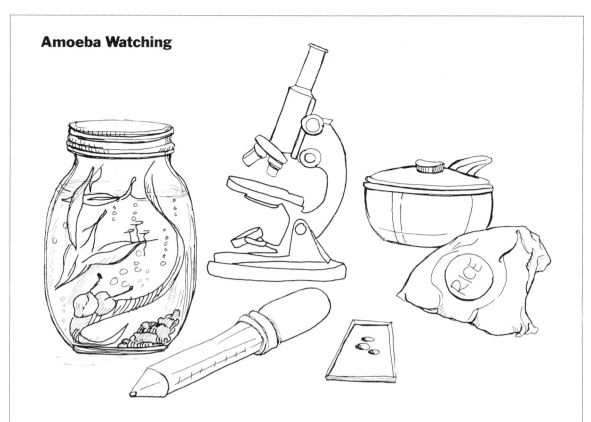

If you want to watch amoebae and other microscopic life, you can collect them at a local pond. Sometimes amoebae can grow large enough for you to see them with your eyes alone, but usually you'll need a low-power microscope to see them.

What you need:
leaves
pond water
collecting jar with a lid
eyedropper
microscope and slide
rice
cooking pan

1. Collect leaves and water from the shallow edges of the pond and put them in the collecting jar.
2. Cover the jar and shake it.
3. Use the eyedropper to put a drop of water on the slide and look at it under the microscope.
4. If you don't see any amoebae on the first try, you might want to feed them so that they multiply.
5. Ask an adult to boil some water for you. Add a handful of rice grains to the boiling water and cook for 30 seconds.
6. Drain the rice and let it cool. Then add it to your jar of pond water. Put the jar aside for two or three days.
7. Put an eyedropper of water on the slide and look at it under the microscope.

One Cell Does It All

Your body is made up of millions of different kinds of specialized cells. Some cells digest food; others sense odors or light waves; others fight off disease.

How do these cells become specialized? Each contains a *nucleus* (NEW CLEE US), and inside the nucleus are *chromosomes* that direct the cell's activities and growth. These chromosomes build each cell to fill its purpose. All these specialized cells have to work together for a complex animal like yourself to function.

An amoeba, on the other hand, has only one cell. But that single cell has to handle most of the same functions handled by the different specialized cells in your body. It has to sense and avoid danger, catch and digest food, and maintain the chemical balance within its membrane (the cell's skin) by pumping out wastes and excess fluids. It also has to produce new generations of amoebae.

You need millions of specialized cells to survive. An amoeba can survive with just one cell. So whose cells are more advanced, yours or an amoeba's?

It Can Live Forever!

When lots of food is available, an amoeba reproduces by simply dividing in two. This means that the two new amoebae are made out of the body of the old one. And under the right conditions, they'll each soon reproduce as well.

Think about it for a second. If an amoeba has enough food and it's not eaten by a predator or killed by environmental changes, it can live forever by simply continuing to divide to form more amoebae. That's impressive!

The Big Ooze

When amoebae first come together as a slime mold, they form a *plasmodium* (PLAZ MO DEE UM). The plasmodium oozes along the ground like a blob from outer space, feeding on minute plants and other organisms.

There are actually two different kinds of slime molds. The *Myxomycetes* (MICK SO MY SEATS) form by combining the nuclei (the plural of nucleus) of all the amoebae into one nucleus. So even though a Myxomycetes slime mold might grow to be a creature larger than your hand, it's still a single-celled creature guided by a single nucleus.

The other kinds of slime molds are the *Acrasiomycota* (AH CRAZY OH MY COAT AH). In the Acrasiomycota, each amoeba keeps its nucleus. Though these slime molds are made up of many different cells, all the cells work together to help the creature survive (just as all the specialized cells in your body allow you to survive). When it comes time to reproduce, each amoeba cell plays a special role in the process. Some mass together to form a stem for supporting the spore structures, while others climb to the top of this mass, where they produce and release the spores.

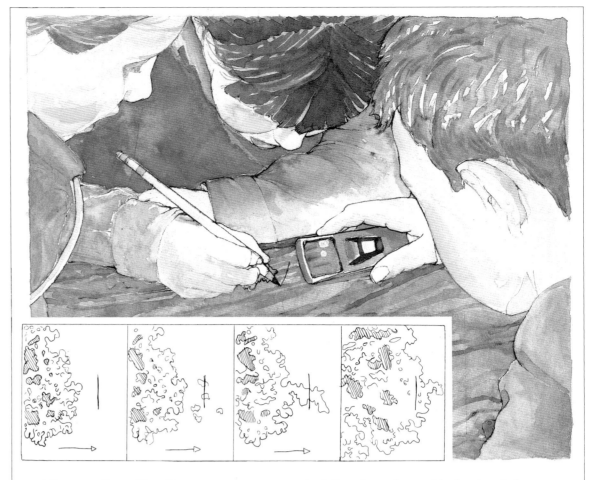

Plasmodium Hunting

The best time to go hunting for slime mold plasmodia is a day or two after it rains, usually in late spring or early fall. The only tool you really need is a hand lens. For even the largest plasmodium, it's helpful to have a 7–10X magnifier to observe its fine details.

What you need:
7–10X magnifier
pencil

1. You have to get your nose close to the ground to find slime molds. Check decaying logs and damp leaves on the ground. The plasmodium is often bright yellow and looks like a blob of jelly.

2. When you find a plasmodium, it might appear not to be moving. Don't be fooled. To figure out which direction it's moving, look for a large (several inches long), fan-shaped growth. This fan is the slime mold's leading edge. On the back edge, you'll find numerous little fingers of glop.

3. If you want to prove that the plasmodium is moving, put a pencil mark a half inch in front of the slime mold's fan and wait 4 to 5 minutes. You'll see something interesting. At first, small bubbles of goo will appear out in front of the fan. Soon, the slime mold will completely engulf the mark.

Slime molds move very slowly—in a full day, they may only move three or four body lengths. They move just like giant amoebae, first extending a pseudopod and then, once the pseudopod is extended, simply flowing into it. Look at a plasmodium's body with your magnifier. You'll see rapid streaming movements inside its body. This is the creature's *cytoplasm*.

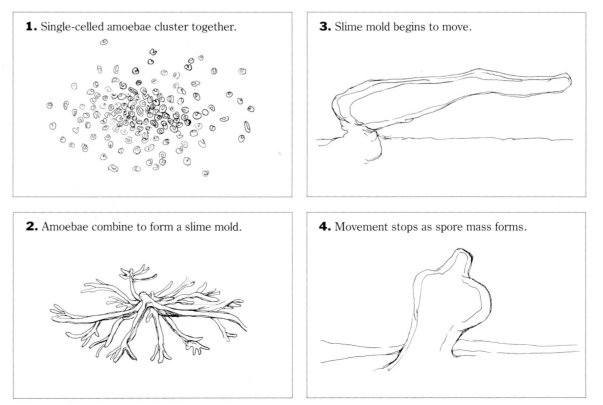

1. Single-celled amoebae cluster together.

2. Amoebae combine to form a slime mold.

3. Slime mold begins to move.

4. Movement stops as spore mass forms.

Home-Grown Slime Molds!

If you can't get out into the woods, you can grow your own slime molds at home in your bedroom! Then you can run some tests to see how they behave.

What you need:
paper towels
small, shallow bowl
dead bark from a tree
distilled water (or tap water that has
    been boiled and cooled)
hand lens
knife
pinch of oatmeal
some vinegar

1. Place a paper towel in the bottom of the bowl.
2. Cover the towel with the bark (cut-side down), being careful that the pieces of bark don't overlap.
3. Cover the bark with the water.
4. Cover the bowl with another paper towel and set it aside for a day.
5. The next day, pour off the excess water.
6. Leave the bowl undisturbed indoors for a few weeks, checking it every couple of days. Add a little water if it begins to dry out. Soon you should see hundreds of different slime molds.
7. Observe the slime molds with your hand lens. How many different kinds do you see? Use a knife to gently separate one slime mold into two parts. What happens to the two parts?
8. Put a piece of oatmeal near a slime mold. How does it react? Put a drop of vinegar near another slime mold. What happens? Try other foods to see how the slime molds react.

Try to keep your slime molds alive through the sporophore stage. Where do they store their spores? How many different-shaped spore sacs can you find? When does each slime mold release its spores?

5. Spores move up stalk.

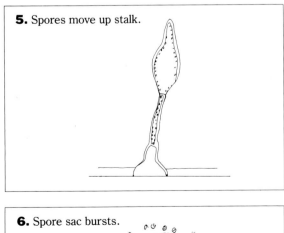

6. Spore sac bursts.

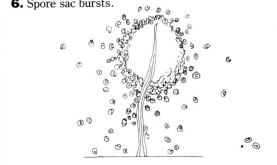

Blob Reproduces Like a Plant!

During its last phase, the slime mold becomes a *sporophore*. It stops moving, sprouts bizarre growths, produces spores, and ejects them into the air. These spores drift on the wind and lose themselves in niches on logs or among leaves. When conditions are just right, they emerge to produce new slime molds.

Many mycologists think this is the slime mold's most beautiful stage. They form a variety of different shapes—stalks with spheres, brain-shaped masses, or fluffy bunches—and they take on a range of colors, from neon green to soft coral pink.

Wherever you go throughout North America, or even the world, there are a few slime mold species you'll find almost everywhere.

Ceratiomyxa fruticulosa is very common on decaying logs. Under a hand lens, it looks like a beautiful colony of underwater sponges!

Greenpatch Kids

Ryan and Gavin Taylor's parents don't mind when they see their kids sorting through the rotting vegetables in the family's compost pile or crawling around under the bushes in their forested backyard. After all, how else are they going to find slime-mold specimens for their dad's research lab?

Ryan and Gavin's dad, John Taylor, is a mycologist at the University of California at Berkeley. Mycologists study fungi and other related life forms. The slime molds that the kids find in the backyard or discover on family outings often end up in Professor Taylor's laboratory, where he and his college students study them.

Ryan is 12 years old, and Gavin is 8. Kids are great slime mold hunters because they have two advantages over most adults: First, they're closer to the ground, so they can spot small things that most adults miss. And second, they love to get dirty. Even as we speak, Gavin sneaks off to crawl under a nearby bush. Soon he's back with a rock. One side of the rock is covered in lovely bright green slime molds. "They crawl up on the rock toward the light," their dad explains. "That's where they release their spores."

Not to be outdone by his younger brother, Ryan pulls a thick stalk of broccoli out of the compost pile. One end of the broccoli is covered in beautiful slime molds. Under a small magnifier, you can see their large spore sacs supported by fragile stalks. "Look in wet places," Ryan advises. "They really like the cabbage and other vegetables in the compost.

"After a rain you should look under bushes where there are lots of leaves," Ryan continues. He holds up a leaf covered in a green smear. "You can't wait too long though. Look, the rain smashed these. Sometimes when my parents go out looking for mushrooms, we find some really great slime molds," Ryan says. "And one time at Boy Scout camp, we found a yellow slime mold that looked like a Styrofoam plate."

The boys' father recalls that his favorite family slime-mold expedition was a camping trip in the Sierra Nevada. "We were in Sequoia National Park, and there was still a lot of snow on the ground. We found populations of slime molds that thrive just where the snow melts. We found a lot of really interesting species. I imagine that kids could find similar ones just after a thaw all across the United States."

When asked why they like to look for slime molds, both kids shrug. "It's fun," begins Gavin. "I really like to look at them," Ryan adds, glancing up from the compost pile, where he's hot on the trail of more specimens. "There's so many different kinds. And it's great that Dad can identify them and use them to teach students."

The Incredible Nose

The long trunks of elephants scan the treetops, carefully selecting the new growth, grabbing the branches, snapping them off, and pulling them to their mouths. While the adults graze on the treetops, the young scurry about gathering fallen leaves off the ground. The oldest female stands apart from the group. Her trunk probes the breeze, searching for a certain odor.

Suddenly, she catches the scent of another elephant group. They're about three or four miles to the south, moving through the deep woods. With a low rumble from her trunk, she turns and heads in their direction. Her rumble alerts the rest of her group. They fall in behind her, ambling single file through the open woodlands. As they walk, the cows use their trunks to herd the young calves, urging them along when they move too slowly or giving them a quick swat when they become too playful.

As she walks, the lead female uses her trunk to check the trail for the scent of other animals that have passed this way. At times she lifts her trunk high into the air to gauge the progress of the other elephant group. As the two groups draw closer, a smelly liquid begins to ooze down the side of her face. Her broad ears fan this odor into the air to help the other group sense her progress.

The groups meet at the water hole in a hail of greetings—loud trumpeting and rumbles. Cows gently touch each others' mouths with their trunks. The young calves immediately begin trunk wrestling and jousting. Everyone checks urine patches and droppings to see where the others have been. The two matriarchs settle in next to each other, their trunks wrapped tightly together. The older cows wade into the water to drink, sucking the cool water up into their trunks and draining it into their mouths.

Aroma-Rama

Elephants are constantly sniffing the air to locate food, detect enemies, and identify clan members. Their sense of smell is a key to their survival. The olfactory sensors (smellers) in their trunks and the olfactory lobes of their brains are much larger and more developed than humans'. Vision, on the other hand, is not very important to an elephant. Its eyes are only about as good as yours.

Every animal uses its sense of smell in a different way. Dogs have extremely fine senses of smell—that's why police dogs can identify and track down people by using their noses. But they only react to certain smells that are important to them. Have you ever seen a dog react to perfume or stop and smell a flower? They might smell a plant or sniff at the grass, but that's usually just to determine if other animals have passed by.

So what role does the sense of smell play for humans? It might be greater than you think. First, all of us have a distinctive body odor. It's not caused by the clothes we wear, the food we eat, or where we live. It's genetic. That's why a police dog could easily tell the difference between you and your sister, but it couldn't tell the difference between identical twins, who have the same genetic makeup.

Smells are important to us from the day we're born. Newborn babies react to their mother's smell almost immediately. What they are really reacting to is the smell of the mother's breast milk. A mother can also identify her baby by smell. Odors play an important role in bonding a mother to her child.

Humans, both male and female, also use perfumes to make themselves more attractive to others. And in many religions, people burn incense or herbs as a way of intensifying religious experience.

Some people believe that a brisk walk in a forest is good for their health. In fact, studies have shown that the odors emitted by a forest contain terpenes, which have been shown to be effective in eliminating fatigue and helping ease stomach problems.

Stop to think about all the ways humans use their sense of smell. What smells good to you? What smells bad? What kinds of memories or emotions do certain smells produce? Once you become aware of smells, you'll see that we use them more than you might have thought.

Soon the young elephants take over the water hole. Some wrestle in the shallow water, while others wade in over their heads, using their trunks as snorkels. The cows watch from a nearby mud hole. As they watch, they scoop up huge gobs of mud in the curves of their trunks and fling it back over their bodies. The thick mud lands with a loud *splat*.

As darkness falls, the elephants retreat to a nearby stand of trees. Two cows sleep side by side, their trunks lightly coiled together. Their young lie next to them in an exhausted sleep. The group leader stands quietly to one side, her heavy trunk draped casually over a tusk. In a few hours, the two groups will go their separate ways, for they must constantly search for food. But they will meet again soon at this watering hole on the edge of the forest.

More Than a Smeller

How does your smeller compare to an elephant's? Can you lift tree trunks with it? Do you use it to talk or to show friends how much you like them? Have you ever taken a nose shower or used your lips to fling mud on your body?

An elephant's trunk is incredibly versatile. It evolved from the animal's nose and upper lip. With its mass of muscles and nerves, the trunk is delicate enough to brush a speck of dust from an eye, but strong enough to pull down an entire tree. It can detect odors from miles away and locate the sweetest fruit in a second. An elephant uses its trunk to show affection and to provide reassurance in times of danger. It's a drinking fountain, shower spigot, mud flinger, and dust sprayer built into one.

Smell Brain

Stop reading for a minute, close your eyes, and take a deep breath. Can you smell anything? Odors surround you constantly, but you're not aware of most of them. That's because your brain suppresses them.

Think about a time when you entered a room and were confronted by a really bad stench. Your first reaction would be automatic—your breathing would stop instantly. But eventually, you'd have to start breathing again, and when you did, the smell would not seem so strong. Even though the odor was still there and the sensors in your nose were still sending signals to your brain, the brain would begin to ignore those signals.

Actually, the same thing happens with good smells. If you enter a room where someone is baking bread, your first reaction will again be automatic—you'll take some deep breaths. But soon the odor will seem weaker. Eventually, you will not notice it.

Here's an activity for you to try to see how long it takes for your brain to suppress smells and other senses.

What you need:
odor producers (vinegar, garlic, crushed
    bay leaves, other spices)
jars with tight lids
nose (any size will do)
stopwatch or watch that shows seconds

1. Place an odor producer in each jar and cover it with a lid. If you're using cloves of garlic or bay leaves, crush and crumble them to release their odors before covering.
2. While a friend times you, uncover one jar, place your nose over it, and breathe in through your nose. Breathe out through your mouth.
3. Continue breathing this way. How long does it take for the smell to weaken? Does it disappear?
4. Try the same process with the other odor producers. Do these smells disappear faster or slower?

Suppressing Other Senses

What other senses besides smell does your brain filter out? If you look at something over and over again, do you begin to miss the details or do you see more details?

What about touch? If you hold a light object in your hand or put on a bulky piece of jewelry, do you soon forget that it's there?

When you dive into a swimming pool, the water seems really cold at first, but soon you get used to it. Does the water become warmer? Or does your body just stop feeling it?

What about pain? Pinch your skin tightly and hold it. Does your body ever stop feeling the pain?

Your brain is constantly bombarded by thousands of bits of information. It sorts through all this information, judges what's most important, and filters out the rest. Pain presents the greatest threat to your survival, so pain sensations are not easily suppressed. Smells, on the other hand, aren't usually too important, so they are quickly ignored.

Trunk has a large area for smell sensors and can hold up to 2.5 gallons of water. Lack of bones enables it to turn and twist in any direction. More than 100,000 muscles in the trunk control movement. Elephants can detect faint odors 5 miles away.

Human nose is only about two inches long and has few muscles. Movement limited to slight wiggles. Odor sensors are concentrated in a 1-inch-square area on roof of nasal cavity. Sense of smell is limited.

Two "fingers" at end of trunk can pick up single leaves or small pieces of fruit. Strong outer ridges grip large objects for heavy lifting.

Hard of Hearing?

In many ways, humans are deaf, and we don't even realize it! You could be standing in front of an elephant that was talking with another elephant miles away, and you wouldn't hear a thing. Yet the other elephant would hear perfectly. That's because much of elephant talk is *infrasonic*—it's transmitted by sounds far below the range that the human ear hears.

If you looked closely at an elephant "talking," you might notice the skin fluttering at the top of its trunk, just where its nasal passages enter its skull. Your body might also be aware of a dull throbbing, something far below the lowest notes of a pipe organ. One biologist likened the force to that of an airplane taking off. Extremely low sounds are ideal for long-distance communication because they travel very far over any kind of terrain.

It is only in the last few years that we've become aware of the wide range of sounds elephants can make and hear. Before these discoveries, we thought elephants were pretty much limited to trumpeting sounds. It just goes to show you how little we really know about elephants, and how much there is to learn.

Elephants aren't the only animals that hear sounds we can't. Think about the times when all the dogs in your neighborhood start howling, and you can't figure out why. Dogs have very good ears that can hear high-frequency sounds beyond your range. Think about other animals. Do some experiments to see what ranges of sounds cats hear.

Long in the Teeth

Elephants use their tusks for defense, for digging holes in the ground to search for water or salt, for establishing dominance over other elephants, even for supporting the trunk while resting. Each elephant's tusks are unique. People who study elephants often recognize individuals by the shape of their tusks (along with the shape of their ears).

Tusks are actually the incisor teeth on an elephant's upper jaw. Can you locate your upper incisor teeth? Now imagine if those teeth kept growing throughout your life! That's what happens to elephants. Their tusks can grow to be more than ten feet long and weigh more than 220 pounds each.

Just as young humans have baby teeth, elephant calves grow two-inch-long "milk tusks," which drop out before their permanent tusks appear.

Besides their tusks, elephants have four giant molars—two on the upper jaw and two on the lower jaw—for grinding food. Over time, these molars gradually wear down and are replaced by new ones. An elephant gets six new sets of molars during its life. Each set is bigger than the one it replaces. The teeth in the last set are huge! Each one weighs more than nine pounds and measures a foot long. When the elephant wears out its sixth set of molars, it can no longer digest food and soon dies.

Greenpatch Kids

Pals of Wildlife

"When animals die, we're all dead meat." That's the slogan that Lyle Solla-Yates and his friends used for their group, Pals of Wildlife. Lyle started the group when he was seven, after he became concerned about the fate of Florida's manatees.

Manatees are large, slow-moving mammals that live in Florida's shallow waterways and coastal waters. While researching a school science report, Lyle discovered that some kinds of manatees were on the verge of extinction. Gentle, slow-moving creatures, they're often shot or injured in collisions with careless boaters. When Lyle learned that a manatee had recently been hurt in an accident with a boater, he decided to organize other kids to support environmental causes.

That's why he founded Pals of Wildlife. Their first project was to adopt a manatee. Lyle even gets to swim with it sometimes! Pals doesn't limit itself just to helping manatees, though. They took part in a Greenpeace boycott of a fast-food restaurant in their area because the restaurant uses Icelandic fish. They marched at a local mall to protest the slaughter of animals for fur. And they organized a newspaper recycling project in their neighborhood.

Each year Pals organizes an "Earth Day Birthday" celebration to raise money for environmental groups. One year, they raised $412 to help save tropical rain forests. They've also lobbied their local senator to support the use of tuna-catching techniques that don't harm dolphins. Adding their own creative touch, they not only sent letters, they also included stuffed paper dolphins to emphasize their point.

Lyle doesn't think he's doing anything special. It's just natural. "If we didn't have Earth," he reasons, "then what would we have?"

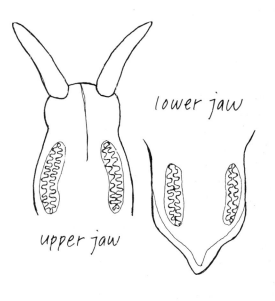

Molar Measuring

An elephant has four molars and a pair of incisors (its tusks). Let's see how your teeth compare.

What you need:
mirror (or a friend)
pencil and paper

1. You have three kinds of teeth in your mouth—incisors, canines, and molars. Using the mirror, count how many you have of each kind and where they are located.
2. Use the pencil and paper to draw a map of your mouth showing where each tooth is located.
3. Compare your mouth map with the elephant's dental chart. How do they compare? How many molars do you have? How many sets of molars do you get in a lifetime? How large are your largest molars? What happens when they wear down?

Think about your incisors. How do they compare to the elephant's?

What other kinds of teeth do you have? What do you use them for? Why doesn't an elephant need canines?

An animal's teeth are a great indicator of what it eats. If it eats a lot of meat, it's going to have canines and incisors for ripping and tearing. If it mainly eats grass and leaves, it's going to have grinding teeth. Think about some other animals and what their teeth tell you about their diets.

All in the Family

Our understanding of elephants has really grown in the last few decades. Biologists have spent years studying elephants in the wild, and all their hard work is paying off. Not only have we discovered the range of sounds elephants use to communicate, we've also discovered that they have very orderly family and social lives.

An elephant's social life is based upon its family group. Each group consists of between 4 and 25 animals. Most have 10 or 11 members, including a matriarch (a dominant female), smaller, related females (cows), and immature calves (both male and female).

The matriarch and older cows play an important role in the group, teaching the younger animals how to locate the best food, find water in droughts, avoid danger, and care for the calves.

The young females stay with their family group for their entire lives. The young males, on the other hand, leave the group at about 10 or 11 years of age. At first they tag along behind the family group, but by the time they are 14, they live independently of their birth family.

Every member of a family group contributes to its welfare. The older females reproduce and provide protection, while the young cows help care for the calves. Poachers who kill an older elephant for her tusks endanger the entire group because each animal depends upon her knowledge for its survival.

The Social Whirl

Let's look at your social organization and see how it compares to an elephant's.

What you need:
pencil
paper

1. Draw a diagram with three big boxes.
2. In the first box, list all the people in your family group. This will include relatives you see or talk with frequently. What role does each person play in your life? Do roles depend upon a person's age? How do roles change as people get older? How do you communicate with these people?
3. In the second box, list the people in your bond group. This will include more distant relatives and friends. When do people in this group come together? What happens when you meet people from this group? How do you communicate with them when you are separated?
4. The third box is for the "clan." For elephants, a clan includes all the individuals in a certain area. Is this true for humans? Who is in your clan? Why? What kinds of events bring all the people in your clan together? Do you like some clan members more than others? What determines how much you like a clan member?

An animal's social organization depends largely upon its ability to communicate. Elephants have developed the ability to communicate over long distances. This allows them to maintain a complex social system.

Humans have developed ways to communicate over much larger areas. Computers, telephones, newspapers, televisions, radios, even CD players have greatly expanded our ability to send and receive ideas. How has technology changed your sense of clan and family?

Bond Groups and Clans

Elephants also have "bond groups" that include one to five other family groups. Though more distantly related, these bond groups often come together to graze and drink. Family groups always greet members of their bond group warmly, while they often ignore elephants from other bond groups.

Beyond the bond group is an even larger grouping called the clan. When food is plentiful, clans of more than a hundred elephants will come together for a few days to graze and socialize.

A Boy's Life

Females dominate the family groups that are the basis for elephant society. But the lives of the young males after they leave their birth family are also intriguing.

Most males leave their family group at about 11 years of age. After a few years of tagging along behind their old family, they leave to travel alone or form small, male-only groups. These groups spend their days feeding and jousting to determine their social status. Each male's social status determines when it can feed, drink, and mate.

Male elephants continue to grow throughout their lives. At first, the younger, smaller males have little chance of standing up to a giant 40-year-old bull. Instead, they wait their turn at the watering hole or salt lick, trying to avoid confrontations as they grow and build their strength.

Adult males keep to themselves, except when mating.

Notice the size difference. female (left) male (right)

An adult bull charging Notice flared ears!

The Mating Game

Most male elephants don't have a chance to mate until they are between 25 and 30 years old. When they are finally ready, they enter a condition called *musth* (MUST), in which they begin searching for cows who are ready to mate.

Bull elephants in musth are an amazing sight. Already twice as large as the females, these great beasts storm across the countryside making powerful pulsating sounds as they look for mates. Bulls in musth behave very aggressively and jump several levels in social standing. They hold their heads high and flare out their ears to look as large as possible. The glands on the sides of their heads ooze a thick, smelly liquid. Their penises become bright green and constantly drip urine.

Cynthia Moss, a biologist who has studied the elephants in Amboseli National Park in Kenya for many years, was startled the first time a huge bull in musth appeared among a family group she was watching. She thought the elephant was sick, and she worried that it would transmit the disease to the female with which it wanted to mate.

Thanks to studies by Dr. Moss and her associates, we now know that musth plays an important role in elephant society. It helps prevent fatal conflicts because only a few bulls are ready to mate at any one time. Bulls in musth are so stinky and so loud, they can easily avoid each other. And because only the older, stronger bulls come into musth, they are the only ones who pass their genes on to the next generation.

Studies have also shown that bulls in musth don't just run around randomly searching for a mate. Instead, cows that are ready to reproduce call them using low-frequency infrasonic sounds that carry for miles. After impregnation, the cow will give birth 20 to 22 months later. This is the longest known gestation period for any land animal.

Compared to You
African Elephant

Loxodonta africana

A bull elephant can weigh up to 25,000 pounds. What's your weight? How many of you would it take to weigh as much as an elephant?

Given a running start, an elephant could do the 100-yard dash in about 5 seconds. How fast can you run 100 yards?

Elephants can live up to 60 years. How many people do you know over 60? Who is the oldest person you know?

An elephant's eye is about the same size as yours.

An elephant eats up to 500 pounds of food a day. It needs at least 335 pounds of food and 24 gallons of water. Measure how much water you drink in a day.

Elephants need a trunk because they can't lower their heads.

bulls jousting

All Thumbs

As the early morning sun creeps over the steep mountain ridge, a loud roar echoes across the glistening jungle canyon. A moment later, a clump of damp leaves, high in the top of one of the trees, begins to move. As the leaves are thrust aside, an adult male orangutan emerges. Stirred from his sleep, the great red ape pushes away the branches that served as his rain canopy for the night. He sits up groggily, smoothes back the long red hair on his shoulders, rubs his eyes, and yawns deeply. He listens intently as another roar echoes down the canyon. His throat sac swells with air as he answers with an equally ferocious-sounding bellow. The jungle responds with silence. Satisfied that he has alerted any intruders to his presence, the orangutan is suddenly stirred by hunger. He stretches, scratches his thick cheek pads, and swings off lazily through the trees.

The orangutan's progress through the jungle is slow and steady. Like a slow-motion trapeze artist, he chooses his route carefully, making sure that each hand- or foothold can support his great weight. His long, slender fingers and toes act like strong grappling hooks, as he alternately swings on his hands and feet while moving through the thick canopy. When he comes to an opening in the trees, he uses his weight to flex a slim trunk, swinging out farther and farther into the clearing. Just when it looks as though the tree will snap under his weight, he reaches out with a long arm, catches a thick limb on the far side, and pulls his body up into the tree.

As the orangutan's swing tree flies back

into place, he has already moved on. His goal is near—a durian tree. He can already smell the pungent odor of the durian fruit. It fills the air with the overwhelming smell of rotten eggs. These large, spiked fruits, which are the size of cantaloupes, hang heavy from almost every branch. Without a moment's pause, the huge ape eases out as far as possible on a thin branch. Gripping the branch tightly with one hand and one foot, he stretches a long leg to pluck a ripe durian with his toes. Pulling the fruit to his mouth, he bites into it, savoring the garlic custard taste of its meat. Sweet, sticky juice drips down his chin, coating his chest and belly. The day has begun well.

Life in the Trees

Orangutans are the most *arboreal* (tree dwelling) of all the great apes. They spend about 90 percent of their time in trees and do not move very well on the ground. Adult gorillas and chimpanzees, on the other hand, spend much more time on the ground. They walk on their knuckles and can move faster on all fours than a human can run on two legs. That brings up an interesting question: If great apes can move faster on all fours, why did humans evolve to walk on two legs? What did this development allow them to do with their arms and hands?

Greenpatch Alert:
Man of the Forest

In Malay, the language spoken in Borneo, the word *orang* means "person" and the word *utan* means "forest." So the name *orangutan* means "person of the forest."

Ten thousand years ago, orangutans lived throughout much of Southeast Asia. Today there are only 20,000 to 25,000 orangutans left in the wild, and they're limited to the small Indonesian islands of Borneo and Sumatra.

Earlier in this century, many orangutans were captured by people who wanted to keep them as pets, display them in zoos, or conduct scientific experiments on them. Usually, these people would kill a mother orangutan and capture her baby. The trade in orangutans has been outlawed today, but orangutans are still in danger because people are logging the rain forests where they live. Habitat destruction is now the number-one threat to these great animals.

The Orangutan Foundation is dedicated to studying orangutans in the wild, preserving their environment, returning captive orangutans to the rain forest, and educating the public.

The foundation publishes a newsletter for kids. They also have programs that allow you to "adopt" (pay for the care of) an orphan orangutan or finance tree plantings to reforest the jungle. If your class is interested in doing a project on orangutans, the Orangutan Foundation also sells classroom education kits.

The foundation was established in 1986. One of its primary goals is to support a research center in Borneo founded by Dr. Biruté Galdikas. Dr. Galdikas has lived in the rain forest and studied orangutans since 1971. She has dedicated her life to finding out more about orangutans. She also works to free captive orangutans and return them to the wild.

As part of its fund-raising efforts, the foundation offers the public an opportunity to travel to Borneo to help Dr. Galdikas and her staff study orangutans. Fees paid by the participants help fund future research.

If you'd like to learn more about orangutans and get involved in efforts to save them, contact the Orangutan Foundation. Write: Orangutan Foundation International, 822 S. Wellesley Avenue, Los Angeles, CA 90049-9963.

Bedtime for Pongo

Do you have trouble making your bed every day? Orangutans don't. In fact, they build a completely new bed every night before going to sleep!

An orangutan usually makes its bed about 40 to 60 feet up in a tree. It bends down trunks, breaks off limbs, and weaves them together to form a springy platform. If it's raining, it will even use leafy branches to cover itself while it sleeps.

How does an orangutan's sleeping platform compare to your bed? What's your bed made of? How does it keep you comfortable and warm? Does it keep the rain off your head?

At Arm's Length

When you try to keep something at arm's length, you're trying to keep it far away. This phrase takes on an entirely new meaning for orangutans, because their body proportions are totally different from yours. Here's an activity that will show you what we mean.

What you need:
ball of string
scissors
measuring tape

1. Have a friend measure you with the string. Hold one end of the string to the floor, stretch it up to the top of your head, and cut it.
2. Hold an end of the string in each hand and stretch out your arms as far as possible.

How does your height compare to your arm span? Are you taller or wider? How about your friend's? Are adults wider than they are tall?

Most humans have arm spans that are about equal to their height. Orangutans, however, have very different proportions. While even the largest males are under 5 feet tall, they have arm spans of about 7½ feet.

Why does a tree-dwelling orangutan have such long arms? Maybe a better question is, why do humans have such puny, weak arms?

Imagine what it would be like to have a 7½-foot arm span. Use the measuring tape and scissors to cut a string this long. Find its center and drape it over your shoulders so that it falls evenly down each of your arms. Where would your hands be? If you had arms like these, how would you keep your fingers from dragging on the ground when you walk?

An orangutan's arms are not only long, they're also very powerful. An adult orangutan is four to five times stronger than an adult human. People say they've seen an adult orangutan rip the jaw off a crocodile!

Look, Mom, Four Thumbs!

An orangutan's long, narrow fingers are ideal for grabbing branches. And its thumb is completely opposable, meaning that it can grab and hold objects.

Even more remarkable, the orangutan's toes are long and thin, too. And its big toes are so short, they work almost like thumbs. An orangutan can cling to a tree limb with its toes, freeing up its arms to grab and hold fruit. And young orangutans don't have to be content sucking their thumbs—they suck on their big toes, too!

Trace your hand and foot on a piece of paper and compare them to the orangutan's hand and foot on this page. Compare the length and placement of the fingers and toes. Can you grab objects with your toes? Try it. Does the orangutan have any protection for the ends of its fingers? Do you?

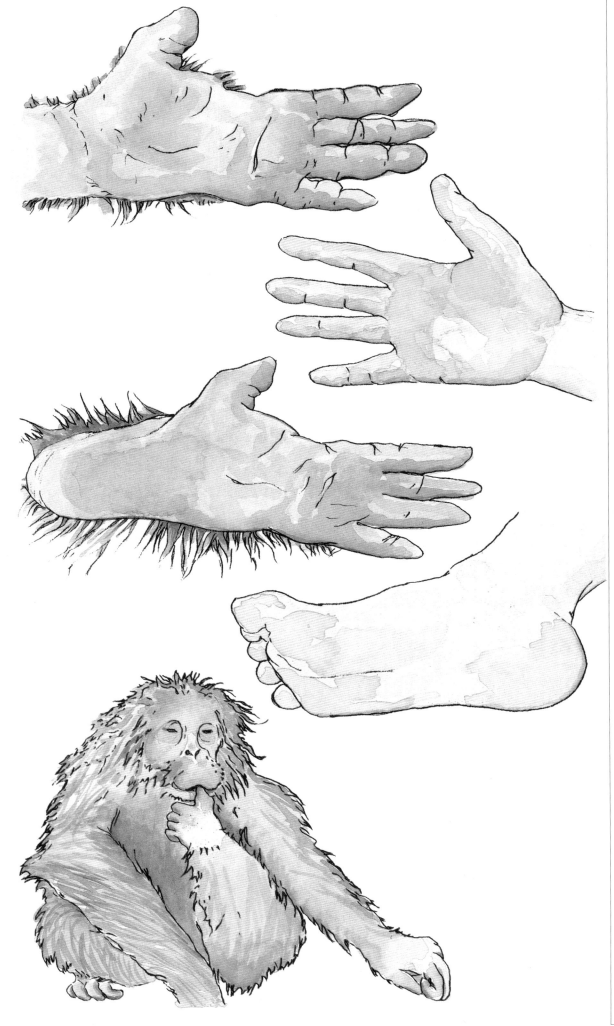

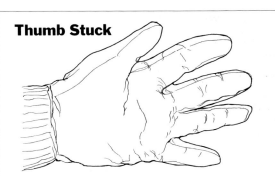

Thumb Stuck

Thumbs are one of the things that set orangutans and humans apart from most other animals. In fact, counting their big toes, orangutans have four thumbs, so they're particularly lucky.

Thumbs may not seem that important, but think about it for a minute. What would life be like without thumbs? Well, firstofall you'dtypelikethis. (How do you hit the space bar when you type?)

Let's do away with thumbs and see how we get along.

What you need:
stapler or tape
old pair of cloth work gloves
assortment of objects
paper
pencil

1. Staple each glove's thumb to its index finger (or simply tape your thumbs to your hands).

2. Put on the gloves and experiment with what you can and can't do. Make a list (that could be sort of difficult, but try it).

3. Can you pick up objects? What objects are easy to pick up? Can you pick up a dime? A quarter? How about a large toy?

4. Can you write with a pen or throw a baseball? Can you type on a computer? Hang from a limb? Eat with a knife and fork?

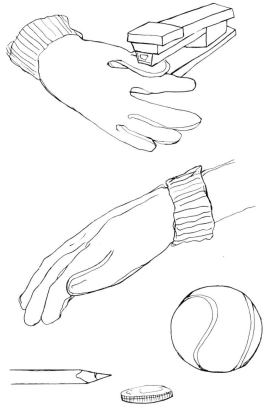

Spend a few hours without thumbs, and write about your experiences. (Be sure to take your gloves off first!) What advantages do thumbed animals have over other animals?

Apes with Human Eyes

One very good reason to save the endangered orangutans is that, along with gorillas and chimpanzees, they're our closest animal relatives. Genetic studies have shown that humans and the great apes share more than 99 percent of the same DNA.

Scientists estimate that a common ancestor of humans and orangutans lived on the earth 15 million years ago. If we want to learn more about our ancestors that lived in the trees, it's important that we preserve the orangutan. After all, it's the largest arboreal animal in the world.

Biruté Galdikas, the scientist who has devoted her career to studying and protecting orangutans, sees another connection. She calls orangutans the "apes with human eyes," because their eyes have whites around the irises just like ours. No other great ape shares this characteristic with humans.

human

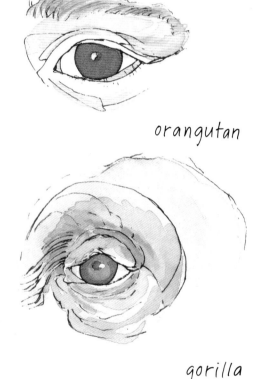

orangutan

gorilla

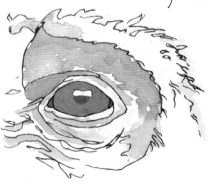

Cheeky

Can you imagine picking a boyfriend or girlfriend based upon the size of their cheeks or how loud they can yell? In Borneo, older male orangutans develop thick cheek pads and large sacs that hang from their throats. Both of these features play a major role in the animal's ability to attract females and produce young.

Adult male orangutans live most of their lives alone. Each stakes out a territory in the rain forest, which it defends from any intruders. Other mature males are fought off or avoided.

The orangutan uses its throat sac to produce a ferocious roar that is designed to frighten off other males and announce its presence to any females in the area.

Once the male attracts a female with its screams, the cheek pads become important because females will only mate with males that have them. Even though males are sexually mature at 15 years of age, studies have

shown they only mate successfully after they've developed the pads at about 20 years of age.

The orangutan's solitary existence helps it survive, because the fruit that is its main food is scattered throughout the jungle. If too many orangutans lived in one area, they would soon exhaust their food supplies.

Compared to You
Orangutan

Pongo pygmaeus

An adult male orangutan weighs about the same as an average adult male human (150 to 200 pounds), but it is four to five times stronger.

An adult orangutan's arm span is about 7½ feet. How does this compare to a human adult?

Orangutans give birth to a single offspring after a pregnancy of about nine months. How does this compare to humans?

Female orangutans average about 46 inches tall, while males reach about 55 inches. How does this compare to the adults in your life?

There are about 35,000 orangutans left in the world. How many humans are there?

An orangutan's diet is 75 percent fruit. How much fruit do you eat?

Orangutan-imation

Long, strong arms are perfect for swinging through the trees, but they get in the way when an orangutan is walking on the ground. When orangutans walk on two feet, they often carry their arms above their heads. Usually though, they walk on all fours, using their arms as front legs.

When they walk on all fours, the orangutans curl their hands into fists. Scientists call this "fist walking." Gorillas and chimpanzees do the same thing, but they walk on their knuckles.

You can see how an orangutan moves by creating your own animated movie.

What you need:

copier
paper
scissors
heavy-duty stapler

1. Copy the frames below. Cut them apart.
2. Stack the frames in order. First one set, then the other. (If you have a heavy-duty stapler, fasten them at the left end.)
3. Hold the stack on the left edge and flip through them. Watch how the animal moves its arms and legs.
4. How do your movements compare to the orangutan's?

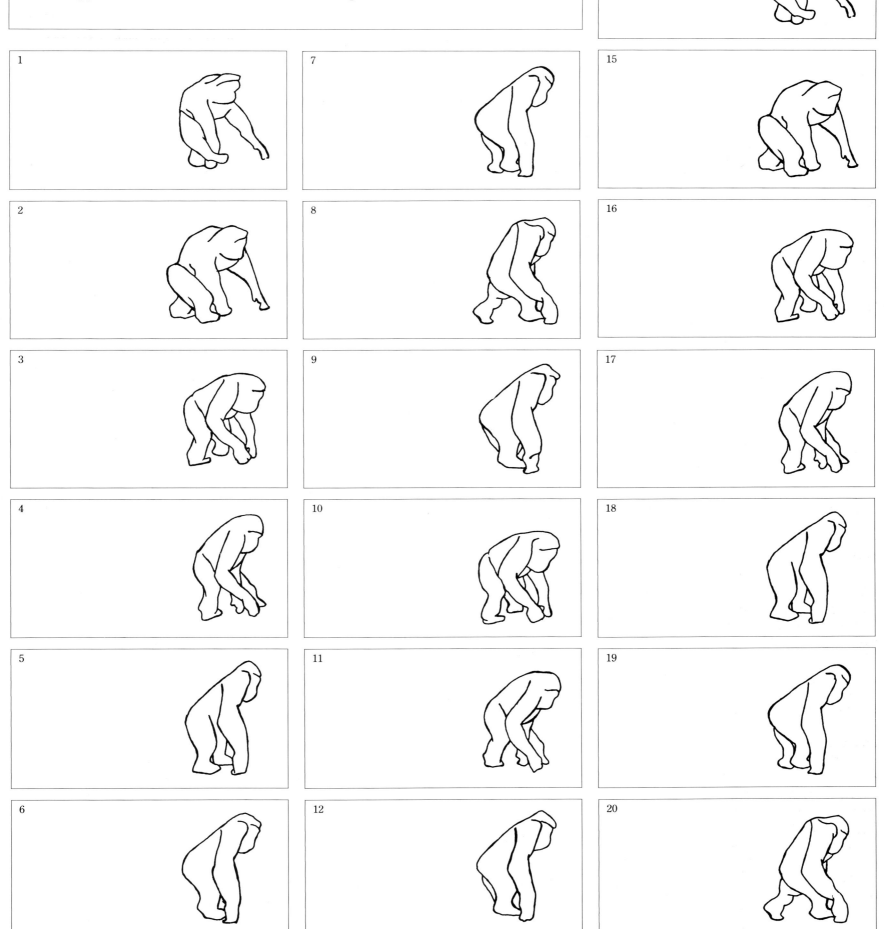

Crushing Ears

With the coming of darkness, the mountains take on an eerie beauty. The evening drizzle eases, and the clouds part, providing brief glimpses of a thin crescent moon. The weak moonlight reveals a mist-shrouded mountain meadow. Beneath the mist, six sturdy figures work their way noisily through the thick grass. A drift of wild boars has been feeding in the meadow since twilight, using their powerful jaws and tusks to plow up the soft, damp soil. The boars grunt with delight as they expose and swallow the succulent bulbs. As the night progresses, the meadow is gradually transformed into a muddy wasteland.

Just as the moon begins to disappear over the horizon, the largest sow stops eating. She lifts her huge snout into the air and begins clicking her powerful tusks together nervously. The rest of the drift freezes and sniffs, their tusks clicking out a rapid response. Suddenly pandemonium breaks loose. Just as the lead sow roars out a warning grunt, a powerful mountain lion springs from a nearby tree. With piercing squeals, the hogs burst through the dense undergrowth at a furious gallop. The lion is right behind them, moving smoothly through the dense thicket.

As the boars reach an open woodland, they begin to fan out in an ever-widening arc. The lion is gaining ground fast now, all of his senses focused on an old gray sow in the center of the drift. He fails to notice that he has passed the boars on the outer edges of the fan and that they are looping around behind him. Suddenly the old sow turns to face her pursuer. With a great bound the lion leaps toward her, his lips curled in a snarl, his sharp claws fully extended. In midair, a mighty blow knocks the lion to the ground. Off balance, he stumbles and spins around. Blood springs from a tusk wound in his side.

Too late, he realizes that he's surrounded. Predator has become prey. The drift rushes toward him. A dozen sharp tusks slash and stab at his sides and legs. The struggle is short and final.

A Pig Invasion

When Christopher Columbus landed in Cuba on his second voyage in 1493, the only pigs in the entire Western Hemisphere were the eight that he carried with him on his ships. Today, wildlife biologists estimate that there are somewhere between .5 million and 2 million wild pigs roaming loose in the United States alone. Where did all these pigs come from?

Almost all of them are descendants of domestic pigs. Domestic animals that have returned to the wild are called *feral*. Feral pigs have been very successful across much of the United States. They've established populations in at least 20 states. What accounts for this pig invasion?

Simple. The easiest way to fatten pigs is to turn them loose. They'll scour the jungles or forests and find plenty of food. The early Spanish set their pigs loose in the Caribbean jungles where they landed. Whenever an expedition was sent to the mainland, they rounded up a herd of pigs and brought them along for food. It was the ultimate in fast food. Fresh meat that you didn't have to carry on your back or track down!

Needless to say, many of these pigs escaped. They're very smart and resourceful animals. They can eat almost anything, and they reproduce very quickly. The Spaniards' escaped pigs established the first feral pig population in the United States. They were soon joined by escaped pigs from the French and English settlers. Before too long, there were feral pigs living all across the country.

Exotics

Whenever animals from one area reach a new environment, they change that environment, sometimes dramatically. In Hawaii, for example, the introduction of feral pigs has caused the extinction of half the islands' native bird species. These birds evolved in an environment with no natural predators—many of them didn't even fly—so their nests and eggs were easy prey for the hungry hogs.

Nonnative animal and plant species are called *exotics*. Humans play a major role in transporting exotic species. We brought hogs along with us for food, and we continue to introduce wild boars to different areas for hunting. Wherever they are able to establish themselves, feral pigs dominate native animals.

A Swine by Any Other Name (Pig, Hog, Boar, Peccary, Javelina . . .)

Feral hogs are the escaped descendants of domestic pigs, but they aren't the only wild pigs to be found in the United States today.

Eurasian wild boars have been imported for sport since 1889. And once again, many of these animals have escaped. (It's hard to keep a good pig penned!)

Eurasian wild boars were never domesticated. They are taller and heavier than feral hogs. They have straight tails, long legs, dark hair on their bodies, and shaggy manes on their necks. Their long, pointed heads are topped by tall, upright ears.

Escaped Eurasian wild boars have bred with feral hogs, creating populations with mixed ancestry. Animals with mixed ancestry are called *hybrids*. Very few pure Eurasian wild boars still roam in the United States, though many of the hybrids look much like the boars.

All of these animals—feral hogs, Eurasian wild boars, hybrids, even domestic hogs—belong to a group with the family name Suidae.

Peccaries (also called javelinas), which live in the southwestern United States, Central America, and South America, belong to a different family, Tayassuidae. On the outside, peccaries resemble small pigs, but many of their features, including their teeth, digestive system, glands, and toes, are very different.

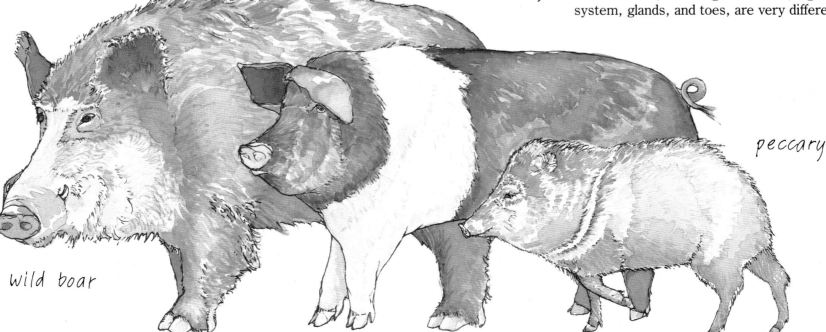

domestic hog

wild boar

peccary

Sweating Like a Hog

How does your body keep from overheating on a hot day? How do you cool off after you've been playing hard?

There are two ways, actually. First, the innermost layer of your skin is filled with tiny blood vessels. When you work hard, these vessels expand to carry additional blood. This blood radiates heat into the air to cool you down.

The second cooling mechanism is sweat. Every square inch of your skin is covered in hundreds of sweat glands. As the sweat evaporates, it carries off heat very efficiently.

Pigs, on the other hand, can't sweat. Their skin doesn't have a lot of sweat glands or blood vessels, so they have to find other ways to keep cool.

Usually, they wallow. They'll spend warm days in water or cool, damp mud. Another strategy is to avoid the sun. In warmer areas, during the hot summers, feral pigs become *nocturnal*, active at night and dormant during the day. What's interesting is that when cool weather returns in the fall, the pigs switch back, sleeping at night and moving about during the day.

Every animal has to control its body temperature. You sweat. Pigs wallow. Think about some other animals. Have you ever seen a dog sweat? How do you think it gives off heat? What about horses and cats? Make a list of the "sweaters" and "nonsweaters."

Bundling Up

When domestic pigs become feral, they soon develop thicker hair on their bodies. In cold climates, they even put on a second coat of hair, growing a soft layer of short hairs under their long, coarse guard hairs. Humans would call this the layered look.

But hair is much more than something to keep an animal warm—it provides camouflage. Young wild boars have striped coats to help them blend into the forest. Adults develop dark, solid-colored coats to make themselves look more fierce. When two boars are fighting over a mate, they want to look intimidating, so they flare out their hairs and manes to look as large as possible.

Humans don't have much hair. Though our evolutionary ancestors were covered with the stuff, it has retreated to the top of our heads, our armpits, and pubic areas. The rest of our body only has sparse, short hairs (or sometimes none at all).

We don't need much hair because we've used our brains to invent other ways to keep warm. We call one such invention clothes.

Hair Talk

For humans, clothes have replaced hair for keeping us warm, but this doesn't mean that the little bit of hair we still have isn't important. In fact, hair plays an important role in our lives.

Did you know that people communicate with their hair? Think about it. Humans send messages to other humans just by the way they comb or cut their hair. For boys, mohawks and shaved scalps send very different messages from ponytails or crew cuts. Some girls like to cut their hair short, while others like long, curly hair. Punk haircuts send a definite message. In some ways, extremely short hair can send a number of messages—either you're in the Marines, you're a serious swimmer, or you're a total rebel.

People read your hair messages, along with all the other unspoken messages you send out via your clothes and body, and they respond almost without thinking.

Take a trip to the mall for some serious people-watching. Think about what people are saying with their hair. Do some haircuts and colors shout their messages? Are some hard to interpret? What does your haircut say about you? Think about your friends. Do the messages they send out with their hair and clothes match their personalities?

What other nonverbal ways do people use to communicate? With their clothes? Their posture? Think about other cultures and how they send messages with their bodies. Appearances can be deceiving, but they can also be revealing!

23

Honers and Rippers

Have you ever seen an adult sharpen a long kitchen knife, rubbing its sharp edge against a whetstone or sharpener? Wild boars have a similar mechanism for sharpening the long tusks that sprout out of their lower jaws. These *rippers* are valuable for digging up sod or fighting off enemies. To keep them sharp, the boar constantly rubs them against smaller upper tusks called *honers*. So every time the boar opens and closes its mouth, it sharpens its valuable tusks so they'll be ready when they're needed.

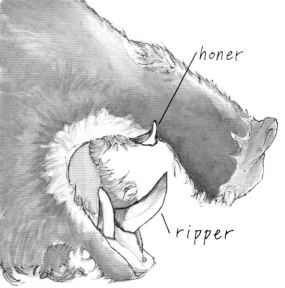

honer

ripper

Eating Like a Pig

Pigs are very adaptable. Even though their ancestors have been domesticated for tens of thousands of years, they adapt to living in the wild rather easily. One of their secrets of success is their ability to eat practically anything. Here are just some of the things people have found feral pigs eating.

earthworms	baby muskrats
bananas	seeds
tree trunks	lizards
plant roots	fish
bulbs	mice
tubers	prickly pear cactus
berries	grains
frogs	snakes
oysters	acorns
thistles	insects
dead animals	crabs
grasses	mushrooms
bird eggs	snails

What's required to be *omnivorous* (able to eat anything)? Not much. Strong teeth, powerful jaws, and a good digestive system.

The Wild Side

When domestic pigs go wild, they begin to change immediately. They become very slender. Fat is replaced by sinew and muscle. The guard hairs that cover their bodies become thicker and denser. Their tusks grow long and sharp.

What about feral humans? Could you survive in the wild as a feral kid? How would your body and behavior change? How would you catch food? How would you defend yourself against predators?

Going Wild

Pigs aren't the only animals that go wild. Almost any domesticated animal can live in the wild somewhere—goats, dogs, cats, burros, parakeets, and horses are just a few. Feral populations of once-tame animals exist in many areas, even in cities where people abandon pets.

Investigate the feral animals in your area. Are there feral cats at the local landfill? Do feral pigs roam in a nearby state park? Call the Society for the Prevention of Cruelty to Animals (SPCA), a local animal control unit, or a natural history museum to find out what kinds of feral animals they know about.

If you decide to look for feral animals, be very careful. *Don't try to catch them or get too close.* Remember, these creatures may look like pets or livestock, but they are wild.

domestic pig   becoming   wild

The Whole Hog

You probably have more in common with pigs than you realize. The shape and composition of a pig's teeth are similar to yours. Its vision is about the same as yours, as are its eyeballs. A pig has a four-chambered heart just like yours, and its circulatory system is closer to being human than almost any other mammal. A pig's heart is so similar, in fact, that pig heart valves are often used to replace defective valves in human hearts.

The list is long. Pig kidneys work like yours. A pig's digestive tract breaks down food just like yours does. Its skin gets many of the same diseases your skin can get.

Scientists can learn a lot about how the human body works by studying a pig's body. Pigs are used in many medical research studies, including investigations of ulcers, cardiovascular diseases, obesity, cancer, and even alcoholism.

Today, researchers are exploring the use of pigs in providing a safe blood substitute for humans. Right now when people need a blood transfusion they get human blood, which is hard to collect and keep.

A blood substitute produced by genetically engineered laboratory pigs would have several advantages. It would be available in large supplies. It could be stored for a long time without refrigeration. It wouldn't be rejected by the recipient's immune system. And it would be disease free.

Such pigs are already being used to produce human hemoglobin, the part of our blood that carries oxygen to the cells. There are still many problems, but if researchers are successful, they will dramatically change the way people receive blood transfusions.

Pig Brains

Almost everyone who has dealt with pigs, either wild or tame, has been impressed by their intelligence. It's hard to judge intelligence in another animal. Do you judge them by how fast they run a maze, how fast they learn a trick, or how they outwit you in the woods? Whichever, pigs score high on all accounts.

Have you heard of Arnold Ziffel? He's a character in an old 1960s television show called *Green Acres*. Arnold is one of the family—he plays the piano, uses a pencil, opens doors, watches TV, and carries his schoolbooks like any kid. The only thing is, Arnold is a pig, a trained pig.

And Arnold is just one of the most recent in a long line of trained pig entertainers. In the 15th century, the king of France's favorite entertainment was watching a group of pigs dance to bagpipe music.

More recently, many of the early circuses featured trained pigs climbing ladders, balancing balls on their noses, riding on teeter-totters, and riding in carts. These were followed by vaudeville acts. One that became particularly famous was called "Uncle Heavy's Porkchop Review." It featured Oink the Singing Pig, which even made it on the *Tonight Show* with Johnny Carson. Uncle Heavy, a 350-pounder himself, explained that he and his pigs didn't need to rehearse because "once you teach 'em once, they know what they're doin' from then on."

The pig's intelligence has played a major role in helping it to adapt to a wide range of environments. It takes a smart animal to figure out how to live in a new place. That pigs have been able to do this almost everywhere humans have brought them is a testament to their brain power. Humans are about the only other animal that has been able to adapt to such widely varied conditions. In that way, we're a lot like pigs.

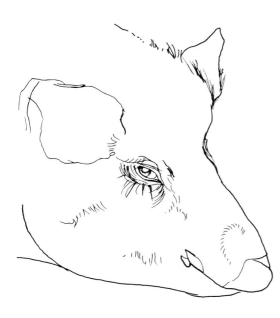

Pulmonary valve: blood leaving heart going to lungs

human heart

aorta

Aortic valve: blood leaving heart going to aorta, which delivers blood to the body

Tricuspid valve: blood entering heart from head and upper limbs

Mitral valve: oxygen-rich blood entering heart from the lungs

Pig's heart valve mounted in stainless steel and dacron frame. Valves such as this have been implanted in humans.

Compared to You
Feral Pig

Sus scrofa

A pig's brain represents about .05 percent of the animal's total body weight. An adult human's brain is about 2 percent of total body weight.

Pig hooves are the equivalent of your toe and fingertips. Can you imagine running on the tips of your toes?

A pig's nose can smell truffles (edible fungi) that are ten feet underground. Could you smell anything buried that deep?

One study showed that pigs on a farm rest 80 percent of the day, eat 12 percent, and play, fight, and browse the other 8 percent. Keep track of one of your days. How do you measure up against this pattern?

Born to Plunge

A cold spring wind howls across the wide bay, whipping up whitecaps on the water. Overhead, thousands of cars roar across a tall bridge as the morning rush hour traffic moves into the city. Beneath the roadway, just a few feet below the cars, an adult peregrine falcon tends three delicately colored eggs clustered on the cold steel beam of a bridge tower. As the morning traffic eases, a slight tapping sound can be heard in one egg. A small beak appears, then a head. Soon a fluffy, damp chick emerges, shivering. By the evening rush hour, all three eggs have hatched. The young nestlings crowd against one adult for warmth, screeching with hunger as they greedily grab bits of pigeon from the other parent's beak.

As spring grows warmer, the peregrines go about their business, heedless of the vehicles roaring by just overhead. From their aerie, the adults constantly watch birds passing under the bridge, regularly diving down to pluck an unsuspecting pigeon or songbird in midair. Grasping the dead prey in their talons, they carry it to a cleaning station on a nearby pier for plucking, before bringing it to the aerie for the chicks. The young grow fast on their steady diet. Each day they become more adventurous. One morning, as both parents are off hunting, one chick wanders down the beam. In an instant, a gull sweeps onto the ledge, snaps up the startled chick, and disappears.

By early summer, the remaining chicks are becoming more active, constantly flapping and testing their wings. With each flap, tufts of downy feathers fly off like small tumbleweeds, revealing rows of sleek flight feathers. The chicks grow bolder, rushing to the edge, flapping their wings as if to fly, and then backing off. One day, a gust of wind catches one chick's outstretched wings and sweeps it off the beam. Helplessly, the bird plummets into the cold water below. For a time it tries to swim, but soon it tires and sinks beneath the waves.

Now, only one chick remains. Almost as large as an adult, it beats its wings and jumps about the narrow ledge. One warm morning, it finally takes the plunge, rushing out and over the edge. Flapping frantically, it manages to land on a beam on a nearby tower several feet below the aerie. It pauses to gain its bearings and catch its breath. Under the protection of the adults, the fledgling takes several short, awkward flights. Only after several hours of hard work does the tired youngster make it back to the nest again.

The young bird's flying skills become less awkward in the following days. Soon it can follow the adults as they soar and circle about the bridge. It learns to flip upside down to grab prey from their talons in midair. When an adult drops its prey, the fledgling swoops down to catch it in midair. A nearby gull colony becomes a favorite target for the young peregrine's diving practice. At first, other birds easily avoid its awkward lunges. Then, one day, a lone pigeon ventures under the bridge. In an instant the young peregrine lunges from its aerie. Moments later it lands in the cleaning spot, a lifeless pigeon grasped tightly in its talons.

Aerial Acrobatics

When peregrines stoop (dive) to attack other birds, they reach speeds up to 250 miles per hour. Even at these speeds they have to be able to adjust their angle of attack to hit their moving prey.

Think about it for a minute. If you stepped out of a plane, you would quickly reach a top speed of about 180 miles per hour. That's approaching peregrine speed. The only difference is that you couldn't steer, and you wouldn't stop until you hit the ground!

A peregrine dives under total control. If it misses its mark or drops its prey after the first hit, it simply extends its wings to pull up, lets its momentum carry it through a big loop, and strikes again (or catches the falling prey). What special adaptations do peregrines have to handle these amazing acrobatics?

First, they begin their hunt from great heights, using their keen vision to locate prey. They usually nest on high cliffs or tall buildings so they can see everything that moves in their area.

When a meal happens by, the peregrine flaps hard or rides updrafts to get into a strike position high above the target.

The peregrine's streamlined body causes very little resistance as it moves quickly up through the air. The light coloring on the underside of the bird's body makes it difficult to see from below.

When all is ready for the attack, the peregrine folds its wings back against its body, creating a teardrop shape, and dives.

As it plunges downward, it steers with its tail feathers. Small bumps on its beak act as wind baffles, increasing its stability.

A clear membrane closes down over its eyes, providing protection while also allowing the peregrine to track the target through the onrushing air.

The strike happens so fast the human eye can't see it. Just before the peregrine hits, it extends two sets of razor-sharp talons. As it hits, these talons rip into the prey's back, usually killing it instantly. Grasping the dead bird in its claws, the peregrine carries it off to a cleaning station. There the prey is carefully plucked before it is eaten.

Peregrines are very efficient eaters. They waste less than 10 percent of their food. How much food do you waste every day? Small birds are eaten whole. Even their bones are digested. Feathers, beaks, and any bones too large to digest are spit back up later.

Frequent Fliers

The peregrine isn't just an acrobatic flier; it's also a very fast flier over long distances. Some peregrines are great travelers, migrating the length of several continents twice a year.

Not all peregrines travel such great distances. Their migration patterns evolved in a leapfrog manner. Those that live in areas that are relatively warm all year don't migrate at all. Peregrines that summer in colder areas just north of these nonmigratory populations spend the winter just to the south of them.

This same pattern repeats itself as you move northward. Each group farther north flies a little farther south to its winter nesting grounds. Peregrines that summer on the tundra near the Arctic Circle fly all the way down to the tip of South America for the winter. How far is that trip? Do some measuring on a world map to estimate the distance.

Peregrines that travel long distances have developed longer wings and smaller bodies to help them in their flight. They're very strong fliers. They can fly at a top speed of about 60 miles per hour, stopping only to feed.

Peregrines are also very smart travelers. They catch rides on prevailing winds and weather fronts to speed their journeys. That brings up two interesting questions: How do migrating peregrines know where they're going? And how do they get there?

Speed Demons

Peregrines are one of the fastest birds, diving at speeds up to 250 mph (miles per hour) and flying long distances at high speed.

Who are the other speed demons of land, sea, and air? Who's the fastest of them all? How do you rank? Here are the top speeds for some of the world's fastest flappers, flippers, slinkers, and runners. These are short-distance speeds only. No animal could keep these up for long.

falcon	250 mph
cheetah	72 mph
sailfish	65 mph
dragonfly	35 mph
penguin	22 mph
cobra	7 mph

Which animals are fastest—fliers, swimmers, runners, or crawlers? Maybe we should give the fish a handicap. After all, water is 800 times more dense than air. Swimmers like the sailfish must literally "fly" through the water to attain high speeds. The fastest humans can run 100 yards in about 10 seconds. If they could keep that up for a full mile (they couldn't), that would equal about 20 mph. Where does that put humans on the speed chart? How does your top speed compare? Set up a racetrack and find out for yourself.

What you need:
sticks for markers
stopwatch (or watch that marks seconds)
measuring tape (or a marked field like a
    football field or track)

1. Mark the beginning and end of a 100-yard course.
2. Warm up with some slow jogging and sprinting. Time yourself over the course.
3. Use this chart to convert your time to miles per hour.

100 yd time	*mph (approximate)*
15 seconds	14 mph
20 seconds	10 mph
25 seconds	8 mph
30 seconds	7 mph
45 seconds	4 mph
60 seconds	1 mph

Can you run faster than a cobra? What would you need to keep up with a diving peregrine? Practice running for a few days. Does your speed improve?

Splat and Poof!

Here's an easy activity that will show you one reason why birds can fly and you can't.

What you need:
two identical balloons
water
bathroom scale (or postage scale)

1. Fill one balloon with water.
2. Fill the other balloon to the same size with air.
3. Weigh each balloon on the scale. How do they compare?
4. Go outside. Hold the balloons at the same height. Drop them. Which one hits the ground first? What happens when it hits? What happens when you drop the air balloon?

These balloons illustrate, in a nutshell, one of the main differences between your body and a bird's body. While you're 60 percent water, a bird's body is mostly air. An adult female peregrine usually weighs less than 3 pounds. The males are even smaller.

Air sacs carry air from a bird's lungs throughout its body and into its bones. Even its skull and toe bones are laced with air-filled holes.

In flight, a bird pushes almost all the air out of its body with each downstroke of its wings. Then it fills its body again on the upstroke. In contrast, though your lungs can hold about 1.5 gallons of air, you normally only expel and inhale about 10 percent of this amount (.15 gallons). During hard exercise, a well-trained athlete might exchange about a gallon of air with each breath. A bird's air sacs not only make its body and bones lighter, they also keep it cool. This is why you'll never see a bird sweat.

As you discovered, it's a lot easier to keep a light, air-filled balloon in the air than a heavy, water-filled one. Body weight is one of the keys to flight.

When you breathe, a small amount of air enters your lungs, which occupy a small area of your body.

Air entering a bird's body fills the lungs, which connect to air sacs. These divide into smaller branches. Some enter hollow bones. A large quantity of air fills a large area of the bird's body.

upstroke: air in

downstroke: air out

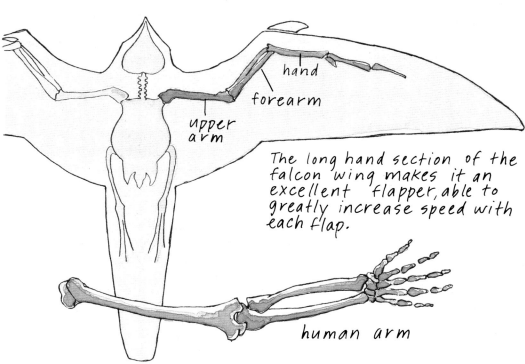

The long hand section of the falcon wing makes it an excellent flapper, able to greatly increase speed with each flap.

human arm

Chest Power

Do you like to eat chicken breasts? You know, the really meaty parts. What you're actually eating is the chicken's flight muscles (though they've been fattened so they taste better).

On most birds, these powerful muscles are the heaviest part of the animal. They consist of fast-acting fibers designed especially for flight. They have to be strong and tireless to support all the flapping required to get into the air and stay there. Nestlings constantly flap their wings because they need to build up their strength as they get ready for their first flight.

Winging It

As you can see from the illustration above, the bones in a bird's wing are actually arranged much like those in your own arm. They even have thumbs!

The bird's upper wing is a single, relatively large bone, just like the humerus in your upper arm.

Its lower wing has two bones. So does your lower arm—the ulna and radius. You can feel these two bones by simply pressing on the back of your lower arm.

It's only when you look at a bird's fingers that the bones begin to look a lot different than yours. A bird has two very long, slender fingers and a small thumb. The fingers have fused together so they can't be moved. The thumb moves in and out to keep the bird from stalling at slow flight speeds.

The bird's wing bones, like most of the rest of its skeleton, are hollow with internal struts. This makes them very light and strong. In many birds, the feathers weigh more than the skeleton. Your bones are very strong, but they're much thicker and heavier.

Another obvious difference between your arm bones and a bird's wing bones is the long feathers attached to the bird's lower wing and hand bones.

Most birds have ten flight feathers attached to their "hands" and numerous secondary feathers on their lower wings.

These flight feathers are remarkable. They close down to form an almost airtight surface when the bird pulls its wings downward. This pushes the bird forward through the air. Then, as the bird lifts its wings, the feathers snap open to allow the air to pass through easily.

Though the bones in a bird's wing look like the bones in your arm, their lightness and the attached feathers give them much different capabilities. No matter how hard you flap your arms, you're not going to fly! Many early aviation pioneers found this out the hard way when their birdlike flying machines nose-dived into the ground.

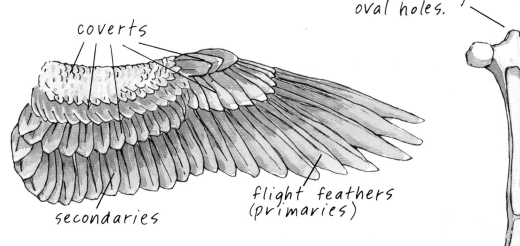

coverts

secondaries

flight feathers (primaries)

Air sacs enter some bones through oval holes.

The fine bones of a bird are thin, with hollow spaces and internal supports – the perfect structure for a flyer.

Upstroke
When a bird draws its wing up, its primary feathers open to reduce air resistance.

Downstroke
The primary feathers close tightly and the wing beats the air, propelling the bird forward.

I Love New York!

Humans have had another major impact on peregrines. They've provided a perfect new environment for them.

Think about what peregrines need to really be happy—steep rock faces with ledges for nesting, open country where they can spot other birds, plenty of small birds like pigeons, and low levels of agricultural pesticides.

Sounds like Manhattan to me! Peregrines are moving to the big cities in droves. And it's not just New York—they're nesting in San Francisco, Los Angeles, St. Louis, Toronto, and a host of other cities. They build their nests, called scrapes, on window ledges and indentations in the buildings. They thrive on the flocks of pigeons and songbirds. Their systems are not affected by DDT, because their prey don't feed in contaminated fields.

Peregrines like the city so much, it's hard to get them to move back to the country. In New York, a traditional nesting site on the Palisades, along the lower Hudson River, is now empty. A few miles away, however, numerous pairs of falcons live and raise their young on the buildings and bridges of Manhattan!

The city has its hazards. Falcons sometimes dive into windows and air shafts, and sometimes they're shot by ignorant people. Things can be especially dangerous for the chicks, because they can fall out of the scrapes. On a real cliff they might only tumble onto a rock a little lower down. On a skyscraper or bridge, they can fall all the way to the sidewalk or into the water.

The city environment is expanding rapidly. Forty-three percent of the people in the world

now live in cities. It might turn out that the peregrines' ability to adapt to this expanding environment will be a key to their survival.

Think about city living for a minute. Just like peregrines, when people move to a city they have to adapt. How do their lives change? What new dangers do they face? Where do the kids play? How does their housing change? Where do they get their food?

Lift Off

Here's an easy way to see the force that keeps birds (and airplanes) in the air. It's called *lift*.

What you need:
piece of paper, 4 by 6 inches
transparent tape
pencil

1. Hold the paper just below your mouth. Hold it lightly by the corners of one end.
2. Blow along the top side of the paper.

What happens? Instead of being pushed down, the paper actually rises. This is lift. Here's how it works.

All air exerts pressure. You might not be aware of it because you've been surrounded by it since you were born. To see air pressure, simply put a paper bag to your mouth and suck the air out of it. It collapses because you've removed the air pressure. Astronauts float in space because there's no air pressure there.

All air exerts pressure, but moving air exerts less pressure than air that's standing still. When you blew across the top of the piece of paper, you lowered the air pressure pushing on top of the paper. That's why it flew up.

Lift keeps planes and birds in the air. The shape of the airplane's wings causes the air above the wing to move faster than the air below the wing. This pulls the plane into the air. The shape of a bird's inner wing is similar to a plane's wing. It provides the lift the bird needs to fly.

There's one more trick, though. Before you can have lift, you have to get the air moving across the wing. This forward movement is called *thrust*. A jet plane creates thrust by pushing hot gases out the back of its engines. Other planes do the same thing with propellers. How did you create thrust on your paper wing?

A bird creates thrust by flapping its lower wings and fingers. This pushes the bird forward. As the air passes the inner wing, it "lifts" the bird into the air.

If you'd like to conduct some more experiments with lift, try this.

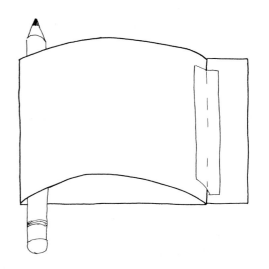

1. Fold the paper so that one side is about a half inch longer than the other side.
2. Tape the edges together so that one side is flat and the other is curved.
3. Slide the pencil through the folded edge.
4. Hold the pencil just below your lips so that the curved edge faces out. Blow across the top of the curved side.

You can experiment with lift by changing the size and shape of your wing. Is it easier to keep a wide wing in the air? Challenge your friends to see who can keep their wing "lifted" longest. Can you create wings that lift up in a very soft breeze?

Coming Back

Humans have had a dramatic impact on peregrine falcons. Our use of DDT and other pesticides drove them to the brink of extinction in the 1970s. The pesticides affected the falcons' reproductive systems, causing them to lay eggs so thin that they were crushed when the adult falcons sat on them.

For many years people thought the peregrines would disappear. They did in many areas, including the entire eastern United States. Then some humans got involved. A small group of scientists, falconers, and volunteers came to the peregrine's rescue.

They began a captive breeding program. At times, they would place the captive-born chicks in foster nests where adult peregrines would care for them.

At other times, if no active peregrine nests were available for fostering, the volunteers would "hack back" the chicks.

Ten days before the young were ready to fly, people would place them in a hack box, a wooden crate sitting on a cliff or tower.

When the chicks were ready to fly, one side of the box would be opened to allow them out. Hack boxes allowed people to watch the chicks and feed them until they could care for themselves. In all these cases, the chicks were never allowed to see the humans, so they never became tame.

Using these techniques, more than 3,000 peregrines were released into the wild in 28 states. Peregrines are now expected to make a full recovery by the end of the century.

While this recovery effort was under way, a campaign was begun to ban the use of DDT. In most areas of the world, it has been successful. The levels of DDT in the environment are going down in most areas.

Compared to You
Peregrine Falcon
Falco peregrinus

Peregrines have razor-sharp vision, eight times more powerful than yours.

A peregrine's heart beats 200 to 350 times a minute. How fast does your heart beat when you're standing still? How fast does it beat after you've been playing hard?

A peregrine's wingspan is about twice as long as its body (it's 39 inches compared to 15 to 19 inches). How does your arm span compare to your height?

A peregrine's normal body temperature ranges from 103 to 106 degrees Fahrenheit. At 103 degrees you'd be pretty sick, and at 106 you'd be almost dead!

An adult bird eats as much as 25 percent of its body weight in food each day. How many pounds of food would you have to eat to match this?

Peregrines have 15 vertebrae in their necks. You and other land animals, including giraffes, have only 7 vertebrae. The extra bones give peregrines the flexibility to bend and twist their necks much farther than you can.

Female peregrines are 33 to 50 percent bigger than the males. Measure your family and friends. Which sex is larger in humans? Does this change with age?

Greenpatch Kid

Birds in the Family Tree

Neil Walton is just past 11 years old, and he's been around peregrine falcons his entire life. That's because his dad, Brian, was a founder of the Santa Cruz Predatory Bird Research Group (SCPBRG). The group was established to help save the peregrine falcon from extinction. They were very successful in their work, raising peregrines at their facility and restoring them to the wild. "We live in an old quarry," Neil explains. "And right next to our house is a big building with lots of rooms for the birds, including really large rooms for the birds that are trying to mate."

Everyone in the family helps care for the birds. "I like to help feed them," Neil says. "The doors to the rooms have little windows so you can see what the bird is doing. So first you check the bird, then you put the food into a little hole and it drops out on the other side. We feed the peregrines Japanese quail. We have a big walk-in freezer where we keep all the food."

Sometimes taking care of the birds is hard work. "I also help clean the cages and stuff," Neil continues. "The floor of each cage is covered in gravel. You get a wheelbarrow and shovel, take off the dirty layer of gravel on top, and cart it away. We have to clean the chick chambers, too. It's dark in there and there are lots of spiders."

When the SCPBRG was established, the peregrine had almost disappeared in the United States. "DDT [a farm pesticide] made the eggs thinner," Neil explains, "so they cracked before they could hatch. This was back in the sixties. Now DDT is outlawed. Even though some people may still use it, things are a lot better than they used to be."

With the peregrine's future looking much brighter, SCPBRG is expanding its work to help other birds of prey. They have kept bat falcons, burrowing owls, shrikes, Harris hawks, and elf owls, to name just a few. Neil is fascinated by the birds. "They're not little house birds," Neil laughs. "They're beautiful and they look fierce."

Neil's dad travels to the city sometimes to check on the peregrines living there. When possible, he takes Neil along. "Peregrines don't build big stick nests. They just need a flat space where they can rest and scrape out a place to lay their eggs. Skyscrapers with indentations on each floor are perfect."

Neil knows the work of the SCPBRG is important. "If the peregrine had gone extinct, they would never have come back. And if the peregrine went extinct, it would hurt the owls that prey on them, as well as the birds they eat. Anytime an animal goes extinct it affects a lot of other animals."

Life in a Shell

The summer sun beats down mercilessly on the barren desert land-scape. It's late morning, and most of the animals have taken refuge in deep burrows or among the scattered clumps of brush. Only a single tortoise remains in the hot sun, plodding slowly through the thick brush, occasionally stopping to feed on the tough, dry leaves. The tortoise has been feeding since early in the morning. His urgent hunger has driven him far from his burrow. Food is scarce. The juicy spring flowers that were so plentiful just a few days earlier have given way to tough, indigestible brush. In his quest for food, the tortoise has wandered much farther than usual.

When the sun reaches its highest point, the tortoise realizes he's in trouble. His heavy shell has absorbed too much heat. The tortoise's body temperature is getting dangerously high. Heat and fatigue suddenly overwhelm him. His protective shell has become an oven that is slowly cooking its contents.

The tortoise begins a slow-motion race against death. Can he make it to the safety of his burrow? The bulky creature turns and begins trudging in the direction from which he came. Nearly blinded by the glaring sun, he plows straight through the heavy brush. The horns on the front of his shell dig deep furrows through the hot sand.

The heat is almost unbearable. When the tortoise sees a small bank in the distance, he turns in its direction. As he angles toward the shelter of the cliff, his body is almost completely dehydrated. Still the sun beats down on his broad back. He pauses briefly under the shade of a creosote bush, gathering strength for one last push.

Each step is a painful ordeal. As the tortoise nears the cliff, he sees that it is pockmarked with deep holes. He heads directly to the nearest hole. It's too small. With his shovel-like front legs, the tortoise widens the entrance to the abandoned burrow. The activity startles a rattlesnake from the hole. The turtle doesn't pause in his wild digging as the snake slithers by his struggling body. With his last ounce of energy, the tortoise collapses into the shelter of the dark hole. The burrow is cool. The tortoise's body temperature begins to drop. He will live to forage on another day.

Turtle, Tortoise, or Terrapin?

What makes a turtle a turtle? And what makes a tortoise a tortoise? First, all shelled reptiles are turtles no matter where they live.

In the United States, at least, turtles that live in the water are simply called turtles. They usually only come ashore to lay eggs. Tortoises are turtles, too. (Try saying that six times fast!) But tortoises live primarily on land. And what about terrapins? They're salt marsh turtles that live along the east and gulf coasts of North America.

These distinctions are true in the United States, but in other places (England, for example) the rules change a bit. Scientists avoid such issues by calling turtles by their scientific names. All turtles belong to the order Chelonia.

green sea turtle

soft-shelled turtle

sawback turtle

spotted turtle

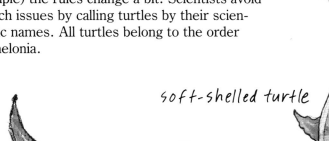

snapping turtle

chicken turtle

Mobile Shells

One of the keys to the turtle's success is its flexibility. Its body may be stuck inside that thick shell, but it's been able to adapt to a wide range of living conditions.

Today, there are 250 species of turtles. They live on (and in the oceans off) every continent except Antarctica. They range in size from the 3-inch-long bog turtle that weighs less than a pound to the 6-foot-long, 1,500-pound leatherback sea turtle.

You can see turtles almost everywhere. They're in your local pond. They're in the driest deserts. They swim in the deepest oceans. They thrive and grow to immense sizes on remote islands.

To adapt to these different conditions, turtles have developed numerous variations of their shelled anatomy. Some species have developed long, webbed fingers for paddling through the oceans. Webbed toes help others cruise across ponds. Desert tortoises, on the other hand, have thick, elephantlike rear legs for power, and flattened, shovel-like front legs for digging burrows.

Some turtles have lost their hard shells. But these usually have a fearsome bite to protect them. Other turtles have developed large, hinged openings to increase their mobility and range of motion. When threatened, these turtles withdraw into their shells completely and hold the hinged doors shut with powerful muscles.

Triumphant Turtles

Turtles may seem like small, unimportant creatures to you, but think about this for a minute. Turtles were around long before the dinosaurs appeared. They were here when the dinosaurs became extinct 65 million years ago (when your ancestors were tiny shrews hiding in holes, trying not to be noticed). And they're still here today. Humans might be the dominant species on Earth right now, but you can bet that the turtles will be here long after we're gone.

In fact, turtles today have changed very little from those ancient creatures that watched tyrannosaurs stalk their prey. Their basic anatomy and lifestyles are the same. Their shells still provide effective protection. Their hard, platelike scales still keep their bodies from drying out. Their eggs (quite a breakthrough when they first appeared) still protect the unborn young.

Frankly, the only things turtles have to worry about is you and the rest of us humans. We keep doing things to threaten turtle populations. We overharvest the eggs of sea turtles. We use desert tortoises for target practice. We build our homes where theirs are, so they have to move.

Fortunately, people are beginning to realize the importance of turtles. We're starting to protect the beaches where seagoing turtles lay their eggs. We're setting aside reserves for threatened turtle species. Shooting turtles is now against the law in most places.

Turtles have been around for more than 200 million years. With a little help and respect from us, they might be around for another 200 million.

Bone Dome

Humans create domes. So do turtles. The only difference is that turtles wear their domes.

The turtle's shell is one of nature's architectural wonders. As a general rule, the higher the shell the better. Not only are taller shells stronger, they're also harder to crack. When a predator tries to break through the shell with its teeth, it can't generate enough force because its jaw is too far open. Alligators are about the only exception to this rule. They can crack even the biggest turtle shell!

You can experience this structural strength yourself. All you need is an apple. First, take a big bite out of the apple. Make it a really big bite so your mouth is open as far as possible. Now, cut the rest of the apple into thin slices. The slices are easier to bite because your teeth can exert a lot more pressure on the smaller pieces.

Three-Part Protection

Turtle shells can be divided into three parts: the *carapace* on top, the *plastron* on the bottom, and a connecting part called the *bridge*. The bridge is notched with six holes for the legs, head, and tail.

The shell can be light and strong because it's made up of multiple layers much like the plywood used to make buildings strong. A number of horny *scutes* form the outer layer. The scutes are made of *keratin*, the same material as your fingernails.

Fused underneath the scutes is a layer of flattened bones. These are much like your vertebrae and rib bones, though they're much broader. Both layers of the shell are made up of many parts, but the seams in the different layers seldom match up. If they did, they would create a weak spot in the shell that predators would soon learn to use.

Because the two layers of the shell are fused, the turtle and its shell are inseparable. Taking a turtle out of its shell would be like trying to take you out of your skin.

Why don't humans have external shells? How does your skeleton protect your body? If a turtle withdraws into its shell when it's frightened, what do humans do for protection from predators?

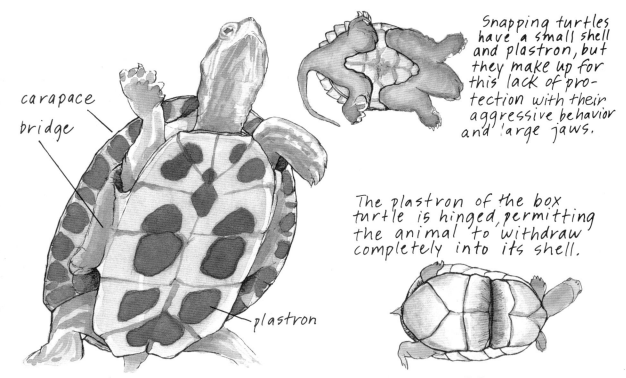

carapace
bridge

plastron

Snapping turtles have a small shell and plastron, but they make up for this lack of protection with their aggressive behavior and large jaws.

The plastron of the box turtle is hinged, permitting the animal to withdraw completely into its shell.

A Dome in the Hand

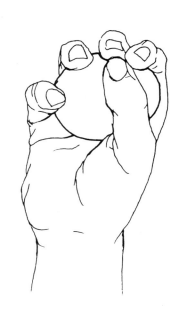

Want to see how strong a dome can be? Go to your refrigerator, get an egg, and try to crush it in one hand. If it is an egg with a reasonably thick shell, you may not be able to crush it, no matter how hard you try. If it is an egg with a thin shell, you may crush it, but you will be surprised how much pressure it takes. (So do this experiment over a bowl just in case.)

The shell's amazing strength comes from its domelike shape. From eggs, to turtle shells, to the roof over the rotunda in the capitol building, domes have proven to be one of nature's strongest structures. It is so easy to crack an egg against a sharp edge. How can something so fragile be so strong?

Rib Girdles

Imagine if your legs came directly out of your rib cage. Impossible, you say, your stomach gets in the way! Well, that's what the turtles had to do to get into their shells. It's an evolutionary trick that scientists are still trying to figure out.

Hey, Turtle Breath!

You take oxygen into your lungs through your nose and mouth. Blood passes through your lungs and then carries oxygen throughout the rest of your body.

Turtles breathe in this way, too, but some species can breathe through other openings as well. A turtle from one of these species has developed the ability to absorb oxygen from water through patches of thin skin in its nose and anus. The turtle just pumps the water in, removes some of the oxygen, and pumps it out again. Using this source alone, those turtles can stay underwater for days at a time.

An Animal Innkeeper

Gopher tortoises are closely related to the desert tortoise. They live throughout the coastal areas of the southeastern United States. One of the most interesting things about gopher tortoises is their homes. They dig *long* burrows. One burrow was measured at more than 45 feet long.

But gopher turtles don't live in these huge homes alone. Once the tortoise is done digging, a whole host of other creatures take advantage of its hard work. Some just pop in to get out of the rain. Others move in for good. The tortoise doesn't seem to mind.

One group of scientists made a list of all the "guests" they've found in gopher tortoise burrows. The list includes raccoons, skunks, foxes, rabbits, opossums, mice, rats, quail, burrowing owls, diamondback rattlesnakes, indigo snakes, black racers, fence lizards, skinks, glass lizards, leopard frogs, gopher frogs, southern toads, spadefoot toads, 32 species of arthropods, and dozens of insects.

Think about your home for a minute. What kind of animals and bugs take shelter in your home? Go through your house to see which animals you're sheltering. What about your backyard or your basement? How many animal guests have dropped in on you?

Shell Games

If you'd like to explore why turtle shells are shaped like domes, try building some of your own.

What you need:
balloons of assorted shapes
wheat paste
water
mixing bucket
scissors
newspaper
heavy objects (large books, rocks)
bathroom scale

1. Blow up an assortment of different-shaped balloons.
2. Look for the dome shapes in the balloons. Long balloons will have a good dome on each end. Rounder balloons will have lower domes.

3. Mix up the paste and water in a bucket.
4. Cut the newspaper into long, thin strips (about ½ inch wide).
5. Dip the strips into the paste. Lay them on the balloon to form the struts of a dome. Once you've completed the struts, wrap other strips around them to form the walls of the dome.
6. Allow the paste to dry. Once it's dry, pop the balloon.
7. Make several domes of different shapes and sizes.

Once you've made your domes, it's time to test their strength. You might need a friend to help you steady the objects as you set them on each dome.

Keep adding more weight to each dome until it collapses. Use the bathroom scale to see how much weight each dome can support. Repeat this with each of your domes.

Which domes are stronger? Higher ones or lower ones? Big ones or little ones? Your dome is the same as the turtle's carapace, the top half of its shell.

Now you can experiment with ways to make your dome stronger. Once the first layer has dried, add a second layer to the carapace. How much stronger is it?

Thicker domes are stronger, but they're also heavier, so a turtle has to trade off between weight and strength. After all, what good is it being protected if you can't move?

Try adding a plastron to your dome by connecting it across the bottom. Does this make the dome stronger?

Try building shells that are shaped like boxes or triangles. Are they as strong as the domed shells?

Solar-Powered Bodies

People often consider warm-blooded (*endothermic*) animals, such as mammals and birds, superior to ectothermic animals. After all, we generate our own heat, they argue. We can live in colder climates. We can remain active much longer. We aren't so dependent on the sun.

But think about it. Ectotherms have several advantages. They don't have to eat so much to keep their bodies warm. An endothermic mouse has to eat ten times as much food as an ectothermic lizard of the same size.

Ectotherms usually live longer, too. Many species of turtles, for example, have been known to live well over 100 years.

You can think of ectotherms as solar-powered animals. They energize their bodies directly from the sun. But you use the sun to energize your body, too. You just do it in a more roundabout way. Where do you think the plants we eat get their energy? In a sense, turtles and other ectotherms are just cutting out the middlemen.

A Real Heart-Warmer

Do you have trouble getting up in the morning? Imagine what it would be like if your body was cold-blooded. You'd barely be able to crawl out of bed, literally. You definitely couldn't stand up at first!

You'd have to wriggle over to a sunny spot to warm up. After a few minutes of basking, your brain would start working better.

After 15 minutes or so, you could probably stand up, and before too long you'd be able to walk. But you couldn't go too far. If you got too cold while eating your breakfast, you would have to take a basking break again.

Turtles and other cold-blooded animals have body temperatures that change with the air temperature around them. They have to bask in the sun to get moving every morning. Actually, the term cold-blooded isn't accurate. On hot days a turtle's body can actually get warmer than yours. The correct term is *ectothermic* (receiving heat from outside).

When a gopher turtle emerges from its burrow each morning, it pauses for a few minutes at the opening of the hole with just its head sticking out. Once it has cleared the cobwebs out of its brain, so to speak, it moves completely outside of its burrow to warm the rest of its body. Then, throughout the day, it regulates its body temperature by moving into, and out of, the sun.

By the way, if you surprise a basking gopher turtle, it will shoot back down into its burrow and use its strong legs to wedge itself against the tunnel. It takes a very strong person to pull a wedged gopher tortoise out of its burrow.

How would your house change if you were cold-blooded? Where would you do your basking? Would you put grow-lights over your bed or open up the ceiling to let in more sunlight? A rock slab might be good, because rocks collect and store heat. That's why lizards love to bask on rocks. Draw a picture of a house designed for ectothermic humans.

Keeping Your Cool

How does your body maintain the correct temperature? Why don't you overheat on hot days? Why don't you get cold when you drink an iced lemonade?

The secret is in your brain. Without your ever having to think about it, one part of your brain, the *hypothalamus*, maintains your basic body functions. It controls your body temperature, heart rate, blood pressure, hunger, thirst, and much more.

When your body begins to overheat, your brain widens the blood vessels that run just under the surface of your skin so they can carry more blood. This is why some people get flushed when they run or play too hard. Your brain also activates the sweat glands in your skin and tells them to release perspiration. The increased blood flow to the skin radiates heat, while the evaporation of the perspiration on your skin cools your body.

Greenpatch Kid

Helping Baby Sea Turtles

When Christian Miller was seven years old, his family moved from a farm in Maryland to Florida. On the farm, Christian had lots of animals, but his new home didn't seem to have any. One day he noticed a lot of dead baby sea turtles on the beach. The mothers had come ashore to lay their eggs on the beaches, and many of the newly hatched turtles were not making it back to the ocean. Christian was very upset by his discovery. He spoke with a biologist at the State Department of Natural Resources. The biologist explained that these were loggerhead turtle hatchlings, and that loggerheads were a threatened species. To work with the turtles, Christian would have to obtain a marine turtle permit that required special training. Christian volunteered to take the training. Working one-on-one with his trainer, he learned how to spot and mark turtle nests, how to differentiate between different kinds of turtles (endangered leatherback turtles also nest in the area), and the procedures for handling the nests. Soon Christian had become the youngest marine turtle permit holder ever recorded in the state of Florida.

Christian takes his work with the turtles seriously. Every year, from May to October, he spends up to three hours each morning on the beach. "It's a big commitment," he says. "Sometimes when the rain is coming down hard and there's thunder and lightning, it would be easier to stay home. But then I remember that the turtles depend on me. Crabs and birds eat the hatchlings, or they can die in the morning heat."

When Christian finds a nest, he carefully writes down its contents in his field notes. When he returns home, he transfers this information to his personal computer. At the end of the season he sends his computer printout to the Department of Natural Resources, where it becomes part of a statewide report on the turtle's status.

Christian is now 18. Over the last ten years, he has saved over 17,000 turtles. "These are the hatchlings I've found in the nest and taken down to the water. When they get into the water, they take right off." It takes up to 15 years for sea turtles to return to the beaches where they were born, so Christian won't be able to judge the impact he's having on the turtle population for a while. His dedication, however, has not gone unnoticed. The Giraffe Project, which identifies people "who stick their necks out for the environment," has honored Christian. In 1992, he was invited to speak at the United Nations as part of the "Environmental Programme Global Youth Forum"; 3,000 kids from 76 countries attended the conference.

Christian often speaks to school groups about his work, trying to get them interested in doing similar projects. "I have turtles in my area," he explains, "but wherever you live there's something you can do. Maybe it's recycling or adopting an animal. Just look around and you'll see something that needs to be done."

Compared to You

Turtles
Chelonia

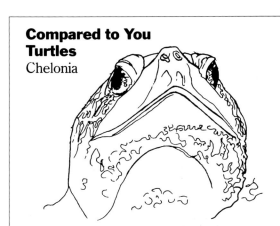

Some sea turtles can swim in bursts up to 20 mph. How fast can you swim?

Turtles have no teeth. Instead, they have sharp-ridged beaks that provide strong cutting edges. Could you chew food without your teeth?

The oldest known turtle in the world is 125 years old. How old is the oldest human you know?

In order to conserve water, turtle urine isn't liquid like yours. It's a thick paste.

Turtles do not have a good sense of hearing, but they are very good at detecting vibrations in the ground. Do you ever "feel" people coming before you see them?

Turtle eyes have only cone photoreceptors. This means that they have color vision and see well during the day, but their vision in dim light is poor. You have both cones for seeing daylight colors and rods for seeing shades of gray at night. Can you see colors in a dark room?

Greenpatch Alert:
Endangered Turtles

Turtles and tortoises around the world are in trouble. More than 14 species of tortoises are on the rare, threatened, or endangered list. These include desert, Galapagos, and gopher tortoises, to name just a few.

Turtles are in the same boat. More than 50 species are in danger, including the great sea turtles. The list includes leatherback, loggerhead, Kemp's ridley, olive ridley, hawksbill, and green turtles. There's also the eastern box turtle, the alligator snapping turtle, and the spotted pond turtle.

You get the picture? Turtles are in trouble because of us. Sea turtles are killed when they come ashore to lay their eggs. And once the adults have been killed for their skins, meat, and shells, the nests are destroyed and the eggs are taken. Even stuffed baby turtles turn up in tourist souvenir stands. If this isn't enough, scientists have discovered that man-made pollutants reach far out to sea in the mid-oceanic fronts where young turtles gather.

As for the tortoises, we're constantly taking the land they need to survive—bulldozing swamps for development and racing dune buggies through the desert.

Turtles have been around for hundreds of millions of years. It would be a disaster if they disappeared because of our carelessness.

It's time for everyone to get involved. Do some research to find out if there are any endangered turtles or tortoises in your area. Check the resource section at the back of this book for ideas on who you should contact.

The Eating Machine

A cold winter storm batters the central California coast. Great waves crash on the rocky shoreline as a herd of sea lions, barking and yelping, plunges into the water and heads out to sea. Their bodies, which moved so clumsily on shore, slide quickly and gracefully through the churning water. Their powerful flippers drive them effortlessly along, and they spiral in acrobatic dives while chasing a school of fish. For most of the herd, it's a routine hunting trip. But an older female, weakened by disease and hunger, lags behind the others. She struggles mightily, trying to stay with the others. Her efforts do not go unnoticed. Soon a new animal appears. A tall dorsal fin cuts the surface of the water for a moment and then disappears. The sea lion senses danger and begins to flail at the water with her flippers.

It's too late. Suddenly a dark shadow shoots upward toward her. At the last second, she twists into a sharp dive to escape the onrushing blur. An enormous bank of razor-sharp teeth misses its mark, closing only on air and water. Energized by fear, the sea lion struggles furiously to make it to the shelter and safety of the rocks. But her strength is soon exhausted.

The shark turns sharply and drives toward her. Again she tries to twist away at the last second. This time she is not so lucky. The shark's teeth rip into one of her fins. The damage is done. The sea lion floats helplessly on the surface, no longer able to escape. Blood from her torn fin sends the shark into a frenzy. It backs off, pauses for a moment, and rushes again. This time, it doesn't miss. The great jaws close on the sea lion's flanks. The shark's body shakes as it tears off a huge chunk of flesh. The force of this twisting blow rips teeth from the attacker's jaw and lifts both predator and prey from the water. The great white shark's sleek body is exposed for just a moment before crashing down with a great splash.

The struggle is over. The shark feeds slowly on the animal's remains, grabbing huge chunks of meat with each bite. A crowd of scavenging birds and fish gathers at the kill site. Once the shark has eaten its fill, it turns away and slowly disappears into the depths.

Homing In

Do you ever prowl for food? Think about when you're really hungry. Maybe you were so busy all day that you skipped lunch. You're still playing late in the afternoon, when suddenly you notice a rumbling in your stomach.

"Hey, it must be dinnertime!" You head for home, but even before you get in the door your nose picks up a scent. Your brain is intrigued. Fortunately, from past experience, you know the scent's probable source.

You drop your jacket at the door and slowly cruise into the kitchen to see what's cooking. It smells so good. Your mouth starts watering. Your stomach is grumbling really loud now. A few passes through the kitchen pinpoint the source—a simmering pot on the stove.

An adult tries to distract you with a small taste. This only makes your hunger more intense. You can't stand it; you're *so* hungry you can feel your stomach shrinking! You're not sure you can last even a moment longer. You move in for the strike.

"No more! You'll spoil your dinner." The voice attracts your attention. The sight of the approaching adult confirms that it might be wiser to wait. You slink off to your room to bide your time until dinner.

Fortunately, most kids have enough to eat. It's not really desperate hunger that drives you; it's simply that you've fallen out of your eating pattern. Chances are good that you'll survive until dinnertime.

Now imagine that you're a great white shark. Your body is loaded with special sensors for locating and capturing prey. When a shark's stomach tells its brain that it's time to eat, the brain puts all of these sensors on high alert.

The Better to See You With

Once a shark gets close to its potential prey, it tries to locate it visually. This is why some sharks circle their prey for a while before striking. They circle in ever-smaller arcs, until they're sure it's really prey.

Many sharks have a special reflective membrane at the back of their eyes to help them see in low light conditions. Cats also have a reflective membrane, though it's much weaker than the shark's. If you shine a flashlight at a shark (or a cat), its eyes will reflect the light back at you.

Dinner Calls

You usually smell food before you see it. Sharks do, too. But meat-eating sharks usually "hear" their next meal even before they see it. Experiments have shown that low-frequency sound waves attract sharks from miles away. Shark fishermen in Indonesia use special noisemakers to attract sharks to their boats.

Injured or sick animals produce low-frequency sounds as they struggle in the water. These sounds travel very well through the water, alerting any nearby predators that a meal is almost ready.

Sharks don't hear with their ears the way you do. They have ears, but they don't open to the outside. Their ears seem to be used more for balancing than for hearing (just like your inner ear).

A shark hears sound waves with sensors that run in lines over different parts of its body. These sensors are called *lateral lines*. A lateral line runs down each side of the shark's body, almost like a zipper. It consists of small holes filled with sensitive hairs. When sound waves hit these hairs, they vibrate. They help sharks hear even the faintest sounds.

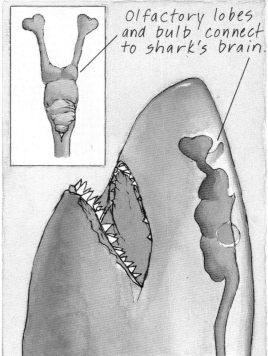

Olfactory lobes and bulb connect to shark's brain.

Smell Brains

Once a shark "hears" potential prey, its sense of smell takes over. Sharks have very good noses. Whereas your nose is both a smeller and an air passage, a shark's nose isn't used for getting oxygen. The only thing it's connected to is the brain. It's for smelling only.

A shark's nostrils are usually on the underside of its head just above its mouth. As it swims, a steady stream of water flows over the nose, carrying with it a host of odors.

Wrinkles inside the nose, called *Schneiderian* (SHNI DARE EE AN) *membranes*, provide a large area for smelling sensors. Experiments have shown that sharks can smell blood mixed in seawater at one part per 10 million.

Scientists sometimes call sharks "swimming noses" or "smell brains" because they use two-thirds of their tiny brains for smelling.

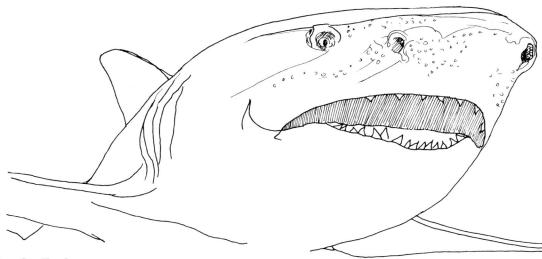

Can You Swallow This?

Because sharks strike blindly and often swallow their prey whole, amazing things have been found in their stomachs. The list includes knights in full armor, a horse, and a chicken coop, complete with the feathers and bones of digested chickens!

The Strike!

When you finally get to the dinner table, you might eat very fast at first. At least, until someone tells you to slow down and taste your food!

As a great white shark attacks, its eyes are practically useless. For one thing, it can't see over its gaping jaw. At this point the shark uses sensors in its snout, called the *ampullae* (AM PU LAY) *of Lorenzini*. They consist of tiny holes in the shark's snout. Each hole contains a single hair surrounded by a jellylike substance that senses tiny electrical currents given off by the prey.

Great white sharks attack blind. That's one reason why they sometimes strike indigestible objects such as shark cages, boat hulls, or oil drums, to name just a few.

Making Waves

The famous ocean explorer Jacques Cousteau once called the environment under the ocean's surface a "silent world." Today, scientists have discovered that it's not silent at all. In fact, it can get rather noisy.

Sensitive electronic listening devices have revealed that almost all kinds of fish (except sharks) make noises. Whales use low-frequency sounds to send messages over thousands of miles.

We missed all of these noises until recently because our ears are designed to hear sound waves traveling through air. When the same waves pass through water, they lose their power. Fish also use sound waves far below and far above our range of hearing.

An Underwater Band

What kinds of sounds travel well through the water? Get your ears wet and find out for yourself. Once you've assembled a range of noisemakers, try making some underwater music.

What you need:
Noisemakers: metal objects for drumming, comb, toothbrush, chains for rattling, air-filled plastic bags, and one Alka-Seltzer tablet
swimming pool, bathtub, or lake
funnel
mask and snorkel (optional)

1. Gather your noisemakers. Lie down in shallow water and lean back so your ears are underwater. If you have a mask and snorkel and know how to use them, do that instead.

2. Experiment with different noisemakers. Which work best underwater? How far do the sounds travel?

3. What kinds of underwater sounds does the Alka-Seltzer tablet make when you put it in the water?

4. The air-filled plastic bags make good noises underwater. They sound like drums and wind instruments.

5. Have your friends try out mystery instruments. Can you identify them?

6. Combine all of your favorite instruments together to make your band.

Now the only question is: Can you clap your hands or snap your fingers underwater? Try it.

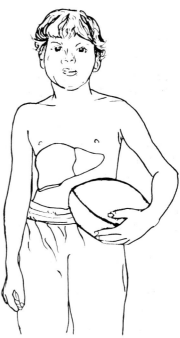

liver, swollen state

liver, shrunken state

Fuel Oil

Sharks are binge eaters. They eat huge amounts of food every time they eat, but then they don't eat again for a long time. It would be like a kid eating 50 hamburgers at one sitting and then not eating again for several weeks.

It takes a special digestive system to handle this kind of eating pattern. The shark's secret is in its extremely large liver, which can make up 25 to 30 percent of the animal's entire weight. The shark's digestive system converts food into a nutritious oil that is stored in the liver. As the liver fills with oil, it expands. Then, when food is scarce, the liver releases the oil to feed the shark's body. As it releases the oil, the liver shrinks.

Can you imagine what it would be like if you only ate once every few weeks, and if your liver expanded and shrank each time you ate? "Sorry, I can't come out and play, we just ate and my liver's swollen."

Fortunately, a human liver doesn't swell and shrink. It stays about the same size all the time. An adult's liver is about the size of a football. It secretes *enzymes* (EN ZIMES) that break down food. Enzymes are substances that cause chemical reactions. The liver also stores nutrients and cleans impurities and dead cells out of your blood.

In some ways your liver is a lot like a shark's. It serves the same purposes, anyway. Fortunately, you eat regularly so your liver and the rest of your digestive system don't have to go through such contortions.

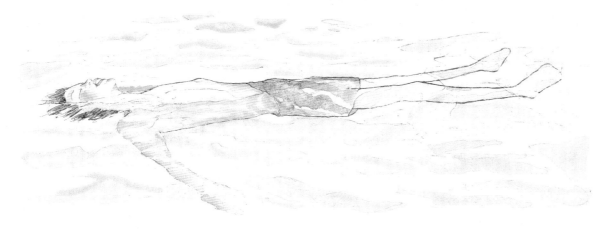

Lighten Up

The shark's liver also has another useful function. It keeps the shark from sinking like a rock!

Most fish have air-filled swim bladders that help them float. Sharks don't have swim bladders. Their livers do provide some buoyancy, especially when they're filled with oil, which is lighter than water.

There's only one problem. A shark's liver expands and shrinks, depending upon how much the shark has eaten recently. When the shark eats a lot, its liver expands to contain large amounts of nutritious oil. When the shark hasn't eaten for a few days, it uses up this oil and the liver shrinks.

Hungry sharks that have used up most of their liver oil lose their buoyancy and begin to sink. One scientist observed that these sharks tend to swim funny. He said they sort

of sag in the middle with their noses and tails sticking up.

Some sharks, like the basking shark, simply shut down when there's no food. Basking sharks live on microscopic plants and animals called *plankton*. When the plankton bloom, the sharks feed voraciously. But when the plankton disappear, they don't eat for a long time. Their bodies feed on the liver oil for a while, but as the oil is used up, the sharks become heavier.

Once it has used up most of its liver oil, a basking shark simply sinks to the ocean floor, lowers all its body functions, and shuts down. It waits, almost like a bear hibernating for the winter.

When the plankton bloom again, the basking shark wakes up, pushes off from the seafloor, and struggles up through the water. At first, its movements are very sluggish, but after it has eaten a bit, it begins to lighten up.

Swim or Sink

Believe it or not, you actually float better than a shark! After all, they don't have an air bladder, and you do. Want to test out your air bladder? Here's what you do.

Next time you go swimming or take a bath, float on your back. As you float, breathe in and out deeply. Notice how your body moves up and down in the water as you breathe?

Your air bladder is your lungs. So take a breath and lighten up!

Humans float naturally. In fact, most of the time we have to work really hard not to float! Free divers pull hard with their arms and kick with their feet to reach bottom. Scuba divers wear weights tied around their waists to help them sink.

41

Built for Speed

All sea animals have to establish a perfect balance to survive in the water. They can't be too light or they'll float to the surface. They can't be too heavy or they'll sink.

Sharks have two factors pulling them down. Lack of an air bladder is one. The other is the fact that their caudal fin (their tail) is always larger on top. As the fin pushes a shark along, it also pushes down.

So why doesn't a shark sink? Both of these forces are balanced out by the stiff pectoral fins on the animal's sides. They act almost like underwater airplane wings, creating lift and forcing the shark upward.

Basically, sharks are built for speed. They don't swim through the water—they fly. Their sleek, torpedo-shaped bodies minimize drag. Their powerful fins balance perfectly, providing tremendous forward thrust. There are a few limits, however. Sharks can stall out just like a plane, and they can never swim backward like other fish.

Repro Shark

Every animal has its own reproductive strategy. Some lay just a few eggs and then protect and nurture them. Others lay hundreds of eggs and simply leave. A lot of the eggs don't hatch, but enough survive to support the next generation.

In some animals, the egg is fertilized inside the female's body, and the *embryo* (the unborn young) remains there until it's ready to be born. Human females, for example, carry embryos inside their bodies until they are well developed. These types of animals usually give birth to only a few offspring at a time, often only one.

Most fish lay thousands of eggs that are fertilized outside the mother's body. These eggs are often eaten by other animals or

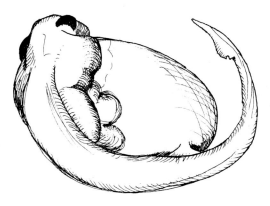

a shark embryo

destroyed by poor conditions. Most never hatch, and of those that do, only a few of the hatchlings survive to become mature adults.

Sharks are different. Their eggs are fertilized inside the mother's body, just like humans. The shark embryos remain inside the mother, often for a very long time. One small shark, the dogfish, has a gestation period of almost two years, the longest of any animal. How long do human embryos develop before they are born?

When a shark pup is finally born, it is already a creature to be reckoned with. Just like a miniature adult, it can bite hard and swim fast. Most predators stay away.

What about human newborns? Can they live on their own once they're born? How long do humans care for their young?

42

No Skin off My Teeth

A shark's skeleton isn't made of bone like yours. Instead, it's made of cartilage, like the flexible stuff that makes up the end of your nose.

In fact, the only bones in a shark's body are in its skin and teeth. If you run your hand over a shark's body, it feels like sandpaper. That's because it is covered in tiny, pointy *denticles* made of skin cells. The shark's famous teeth are simply enlarged denticles that are attached to the animal's jaws.

Meat-eating sharks have several rows of teeth growing at once. If any teeth fall out when the shark strikes its prey (a common occurrence), they are replaced in a few days. Do you remember how long it took you to replace your baby teeth when they fell out?

Sharks often use their rough skin to check out an injured animal. They brush against it, causing it to bleed. The shark's skin sensors then tell it whether or not the animal would make a good meal.

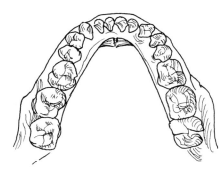

great white shark tooth (actual size)

What's Eating You?

Speaking of teeth, sharks receive a lot of bad press for their diet. Specifically, the fact that it sometimes includes humans.

But think about this: Of the more than 350 different species of shark, only about 25 have ever been involved in an attack on a human. In fact, though this is little consolation for swimmers who find themselves confronting a shark, we eat a lot more of them than they eat of us.

Compared to You
Great White Shark

Carcharodon carcharias

A shark uses more than 20,000 teeth in a lifetime. How many will you use in your lifetime? Don't guess, count them.

Some sharks can bite down with a force of 18 tons per square inch. How much force do you think it takes you to bite into a steak or a crisp apple?

A 6-foot-long shark has an intestine that is about 6 feet long. A 6-foot-tall person has an intestine that is 32 feet long. Your intestines curl around inside your stomach, providing a large surface area for digesting food.

Remoras are fish that attach themselves to the sides of sharks, living on leftover food scraps. What animals associate themselves with humans in the same way?

There are more than 350 species of shark, ranging from 60-foot-long whale sharks (the biggest fish in the sea) to 12-inch-long dwarf sharks. How many species of humans are there? How varied are we?

Greenpatch Kids

Animals Rehabilitating Kids (ARK)

In 1974, Sam Chattin, a teacher at William H. English Middle School in Scottsburg, Indiana, brought an injured snake into his classroom to try to get his seventh- and eighth-grade students interested in science. It worked. Soon people were bringing in injured animals from all over Indiana and neighboring states for the children to rehabilitate. Today, their program, known as ARK, is the largest wildlife rehabilitation facility in a three-state area. They care for hundreds of animals each year, most of which are birds of prey. The program is a great success on all levels: students' test scores in science are astronomical; the ARK program has received national attention; and, naturally, the students love science.

The best part about ARK is that the students take responsibility for the animals. They run the refuge, not their teacher. They examine the animals, treat them, and release them back into the wild. A local veterinarian volunteers his services when an animal requires medical treatment or medication. And if an animal is beyond help and all resources have been exhausted, the students will make the tough decision to kill it. Other animals that can't be returned to the wild are used in the program's educational outreach presentations.

The animals, which the students call "brother" and "sister," are the teachers in this classroom. They teach the students responsibility. They spur them on to ask more questions and investigate issues more deeply. They teach them respect for life. They give the students expertise and information that has given them the opportunity to travel across the country talking to executives at chemical companies about toxic spills, testifying in court about animal abuse, and lobbying for animal rights legislation. The students have also given programs in 47 states, as well as in England, West Germany, Israel, and Russia.

If you'd like to get more information on the program, or if you need advice on how to handle injured wildlife, you can contact the program at The ARK Project, William H. English Middle School, South 3rd Street, Scottsburg, IN 47170. Include $2 to cover duplication and postage.

Brandy Chandler is an eighth grader in Mr. Chattin's science class at William H. English Middle School. She's taken a special course and is now helping with the animals in the ARK program. She and her classmates have developed some simple advice for handling wild animals that might be injured or abandoned.

"If you find a baby and you don't see the father or mother," she begins, "don't mess with them. The adults can be gone for a long period of time. They'll probably come back. So stay away unless you see a dead mother."

Brandy also warns that you shouldn't approach injured mammals. "Always think of your safety first. They could harbor rabies, which you can catch if they bite or scratch you. The safest thing to do is call the police, a game warden, or animal control. They know how to handle wild animals safely and where to take them for help."

In most cases, it's much safer to approach an injured bird. "We can't catch any diseases from birds," Brandy explains. "If you find an injured bird, the first thing you should do is put it in a dark box so it can calm down. If you don't have a box, cover its head so it can't see you. This way it won't panic. Just make sure that it can still breathe through the cloth. Once the bird is calm you can check it out. Gently feel its wings to see if they're broken. If it's a small bird, put your finger at the bottom of its claw. If it grabs your finger that means its leg isn't broken. With larger birds, you can do the same thing with a stick. If its legs or wings are broken, you'll need to get it to a veterinarian or an animal rehabilitation facility like ours. Don't plan to raise a bird, because it will get imprinted with the image of humans and it will learn to depend on us for food. Then it will never be able to return to the wild. If you have to keep a bird or chick while it heals, you should feed it a special food. We feed our chicks ¾ cup of dry cat food mixed with ¼ cup of water. Let the cat food soak until it's soft. Then offer it to the bird with tweezers. You don't have to worry about liquids. The bird will get enough moisture as it feeds."

Brandy and her classmates see all kinds of injured animals from birds (owls, kestrels, and cardinals) to snakes and small mammals. From the moment they receive an animal, their goal is to get it ready to return to the wild. She especially likes to work with the birds of prey. "Before we release them, we have to make sure they have good flight. We have special equipment and facilities where they can practice flying on a long leash. Once the birds start soaring, we know that they're going to make it. We even put out mice so they can practice hunting. It's really exciting."

Resources

Elephants

Echo of the Elephants by Cynthia Moss, New York: William Morrow and Company, 1994.

Elephant Memories by Cynthia Moss, New York: William Morrow and Company, 1988. Cynthia Moss's research has revolutionized our understanding of elephants.

Elephants by Eric S. Grace, San Francisco: Sierra Club Books, 1993. Great for kids.

"Elephant Memories." This National Geographic video provides a beautiful and scientifically accurate portrait of African elephants. Check for it in your local library or video store.

Orangutans

"Search for the Great Ape." This video, produced by the National Geographic Society in 1975, follows the fieldwork of orangutan researcher Dr. Biruté Galdikas and mountain gorilla researcher Dian Fossey. It captures the excitement and difficulties of fieldwork in the jungles of central Africa and the Indonesian island of Borneo. Available at local libraries, or from Vestron Video, P.O. Box 10382, Stamford, CT 06901.

Walking with the Great Apes by Sy Montgomery, Boston: Houghton Mifflin Company, 1991. This book tells the inspiring stories of the revolutionary primate research conducted by Jane Goodall, Dian Fossey, and Biruté Galdikas. It focuses on the special skills that these women brought to their research.

Orangutan Foundation International, 822 S. Wellesley Ave., Los Angeles, CA 90049-9963. This foundation is dedicated to orangutan research, education, and preservation. The foundation offers trips, educational programs, and materials. One primary focus is returning captive orangutans to the wild and restoring the rain forest.

Feral Pigs

Wild Boars by Darrel Nicholson, Minneapolis: Carolrhoda Books, 1987. An excellent children's book.

Wild Pigs of the United States by John Mayer and I. Lehr Brisbin Jr., Athens: University of Georgia Press, 1991.

The Hog Book by William Hedgepeth, New York: Doubleday & Company, 1978. A delightful book, part yarn and part scientific treatise, that explores every aspect of piggery, from how to tell a pig from a kangaroo to the pig circus acts of the past.

Peregrine Falcons

Hawk Mountain Sanctuary Association. Each fall, thousands of migrating raptors pass over this mountainous area of eastern Pennsylvania. In 1934, a group of conservationists established the area as the world's first birds-of-prey sanctuary. Today, thousands of people journey to Hawk Mountain to watch the hawks. If you live in the area, try to visit. If you would simply like more information on a specific bird of prey, contact them at RD2, Box 191, Kempton, PA 19529. Their phone number is 610-756-6961.

The Peregrine Fund. Initially established to spearhead the recovery of the peregrine falcon, this group is now working to save other bird populations as well. They've established a World Center for Birds of Prey in Boise, Idaho, where they breed endangered birds and direct a worldwide research and restoration program. The center also offers public exhibits and programs for schoolchildren. Their address is 5666 West Flying Hawk Lane, Boise, ID 83709. Their phone number is 208-362-3716.

Turtles

Desert Tortoise Preserve Committee, P.O. Box 2910, San Bernardino, CA 92406. 714-884-9700. This group formed in 1974 to help preserve the endangered desert tortoise. They are helping to raise money for land acquisitions and raise awareness through education efforts.

California Turtle and Tortoise Club, Westchester Chapter, P.O. Box 90252, Los Angeles, CA 90009. This is a group for people who are dedicated to the conservation of turtles, tortoises, and their habitat. They do not believe that young children should have turtles as pets because they might harm them. Turtles should also never be taken from the wild. If, however, you have a question about the care, feeding, or housing of a turtle already in captivity, they probably have the information you need. You might want to become a member and receive the very informative *Tortuga Gazette* or attend their annual Turtle and Tortoise Show held each year in June.

If you'd like information about the turtles and tortoises in your area, try contacting the State Department of Fish and Game. They probably have an expert on staff who can help you find out more. Also, many communities have local herpetological societies. Ask around at your neighborhood pet store.

The Amateur Zoologist's Guide to Turtles and Crocodilians by Robert Zappalorti, Harrisburg, PA: Stackpole Books, 1976. A good introduction to the different groups of turtles and tortoises.

Honoring Environmental Heroes
The Giraffe Project

This group's aim is to honor people who "stick their necks out" for the common good. As they say in their statement of purpose, "The Giraffe Project has been moving people into caring, courageous action since 1982. Its strategy is simple: If you want someone to take a risk for others' well-being, show them someone else going first. The Giraffe Project has been finding them and telling their stories through the mass media since its founding."

The great thing about the project is that they'll recognize people of any age, as long as they've stood up for something good, like the environment. Two of the Greenpatch Kids in this book are "giraffes." The program has developed information on about 800 "giraffes" all over the country. They give this information to newspapers and television networks across the country, who turn it into articles and stories. By getting these stories out, the project hopes to encourage others to take initiative.

The Giraffe Project also offers a classroom program, Standing Tall, which helps build courage, caring, and responsibility in kids from 6 to 18 years old. If you'd like to bring one of your "local heroes" to the project's attention, or if you'd just like more information about their programs, write to them at P.O. Box 799, Langley, WA 98260. Their phone number is 206-221-7989 for the main office, and 206-221-0757 for the education program.

On the Wing

Most people don't realize it, but each year millions of *raptors* (a group that includes falcons, hawks, eagles, vultures, and other birds of prey) are on the move right over their heads. These migrations only become noticeable in areas where mountain ranges, large masses of water, and wind currents funnel all the birds into a small area. At the Panama Canal, for example, more than 2.5 million raptors were counted in one season. And these were only the birds that could be seen from the ground! Many migratory birds fly so high that they're hidden in the clouds.

If you can't make it to the Panama Canal, there are a number of places in the United States where migrating raptors are concentrated. Here are a few of the busiest sites:

Point Diablo, California
Marin Headlands, California
Duluth, Minnesota
Goshute Mountains, Nevada
Cape May Point, New Jersey
Hawk Mountain, Pennsylvania
Cedar Grove, Wisconsin

These are just a few of the best areas. Tens of thousands of raptors fly over each autumn on their way south, and again in the spring on their return trips. If you live near one of these areas, it's well worth planning a day trip. Ask around to see if local bird groups or museums offer guided trips.

All you need for raptor-watching are a good pair of binoculars and a bird identification book that has good illustrations of birds of prey.

If you don't live near one of the areas listed and still want to see migrating raptors, contact a local museum, natural history society, or parks department to see if there are any places in your area where birds congregate. Autumn and spring are great times for bird-watching because all kinds of birds are on the wing. With a little investigation, you'll make some surprising finds.

Glossary

Acrasiomycota a type of slime mold.

aerie a bird of prey's nest.

amoeba a microscopic single-celled creature that moves by changing its shape.

ampullae of Lorenzini special sensors in a shark's snout that detect weak electrical currents.

arboreal living in, or associated with, trees.

bond group in elephants, a loose association of related family groups.

carapace the part of a turtle's shell that protects its back.

caudal fin the vertical fin that forms a fish's tail.

chromosomes threadlike bodies in a cell's nucleus that contain the genes.

circulatory system the heart, blood, and blood vessels that transport food, oxygen, and wastes through a body.

clan all of the elephants living in a particular area.

cones receptors in the iris of the eye that detect color, produce sharp images, and help you see in bright light.

cytoplasm the fluid inside a cell's membrane or outer wall.

denticles a shark's bony skin cells.

diurnal animals that are active during the day.

domesticate the process of taming a wild animal.

ectotherm an animal whose body temperature changes with the temperature of the environment.

embryo a fertilized egg in its early stages of development inside its mother's womb.

endotherm an animal that generates its own body heat.

enzymes substances that produce chemical reactions.

exotic species animals and plants that have been brought in from other areas.

feral domesticated animals that return to the wild.

fungi the plural of fungus, a group that includes mushrooms, molds, and mildews.

gestation the period of time a fertilized egg is carried in its mother's womb.

gills organs for getting oxygen out of water.

gular horn growths that stick out from the front of a desert tortoise's shell.

hybrid the young produced by interbreeding between members of different species.

hypothalamus the part of the brain that controls basic (involuntary) body functions like blood pressure, heart rate, and body temperature.

incisors the sharp cutting teeth in the front of your jaw.

infrasonic sounds that are below the range of human hearing.

lateral line a row of sensors that runs down the sides of a fish's body.

lift the force that moves an object upward off the ground.

matriarch the lead female in an elephant family group.

migrate to move periodically from one area to another. Some animals migrate long distances every year.

milk tusks a young elephant's temporary "baby tusks," which fall out and are replaced by permanent tusks as they grow older.

molars the grinding teeth in the back of your jaw.

musth a state male elephants reach when they are ready to mate.

mycologist a scientist who studies fungi and related organisms.

Myxomycetes a kind of slime mold.

nocturnal animals who are active at night.

nucleus the part of a cell that controls its development.

olfactory lobe the part of the brain that detects smells.

olfactory sensors nerve cells that detect smells.

omnivore an animal that eats all kinds of food, both animal and plant.

pectoral fin the horizontal fins on either side of a fish's body.

pesticides chemicals used to kill animals that humans consider pests.

plankton small, often microscopic organisms that float in still or moving freshwater, or in salt water.

plasmodium a slime mold's mobile stage.

plastron the part of a turtle's shell that protects its stomach.

pseudopods an amoeba's "false foot," which it uses for movement and feeding.

radius a lower arm bone.

raptors birds of prey, such as falcons, eagles, and vultures.

rods receptors in the eye that detect motion in low light conditions.

Schneiderian membranes wrinkles in a shark's nose that increase its smelling capabilities.

scutes the horny outer layer of a turtle's shell.

sporophore a slime mold's reproductive stage.

thrust forward movement that creates lift so objects and animals can fly.

ulna a lower arm bone.

ultrasonic sounds that are higher than the range of human hearing.

Acknowledgments

This book is dedicated to Jessie, my Greenpatch Kid. Many thanks to everyone who helped me, including Barbara Ando, Reg and Kathy Barrett, Cathy Berger Kaye, Sam Chattin, Gigi Dornfest, Mark Goodwin, Howard Hutchison, Norman Kurtin, John McCosker, Jim Robertson, Howard Steinman, John Taylor, Brian Walton, and Eve Watts.

> ## Greenpatch Alert:
> ### Endangered African Elephants
>
> African elephants are disappearing fast! In the early 1970s, Tanzania had 250,000 elephants. By 1990, the population had been reduced to 55,000. During the 1980s, 70 percent of the elephants living in Kenya were killed. Similar killings occurred in country after country. In 1989, one writer calculated that 300 African elephants were dying every day. What caused this massacre? Human greed.
>
> Ivory poachers were killing the elephants for their tusks. People in the richer countries of Asia, Europe, and North America prized beautifully carved ivory figures. By African standards, poachers could make a fortune providing tusks to these markets.
>
> The massive killings continued until 1989 when the international ivory trade was banned. The peace, however, is very fragile. Some countries are already beginning to argue that the elephant's status should be "downlisted" from endangered to threatened. They want to begin trading elephant products, such as hides and meat (though not ivory). So far their arguments have been defeated, but who knows for how long.
>
> The elephants also face another even greater threat. Africa's human population is growing out of control. Elephants need a lot of land to survive. As the human population grows, villages and farms fill the open spaces once occupied by elephants. Confined to ever-smaller areas, the elephants destroy the environment and come into conflict with local farmers.
>
> The elephant's fate is still undecided. The ivory trade may come back to life. The human population bomb is ticking ever faster. If you and your friends would like to help protect Africa's elephants, you can adopt an elephant family in Kenya's Amboseli National Park. The adoption program is sponsored by Elefriends, part of England's Born Free Foundation. The group uses the money it raises to fight the ivory trade and to support the rangers who protect the elephants from poachers. In the United States, you can get more information on Elefriends by contacting The Overlook Press, 2568 Route 212, Woodstock, NY 12498.

Index

SMALL CAPITALS indicate activities or projects.

Scientific Classifications

Scientists have identified almost two million plants and animals. And people are discovering more every day!

To keep everything straight, scientists use a system that divides animals, plants, and other creatures into groups, depending upon how they are built. Organisms with similar structures are put together in one group, while those with very different structures go into other groups.

Scientists use this system to divide and subdivide living things into smaller and smaller groups depending upon how much alike they are. If two animals are identical down to the species (the smallest group), they are very closely related. If two animals are in different phyla (large groups), they are quite different from each other.

Here are the different divisions, and how you fit into the scheme of things: There are five **kingdoms**, the broadest classification. These include plants, animals, fungi (mushrooms), protists (protozoa and algae), and monera (bacteria). Humans are animals, so you belong in that group.

The animal kingdom is divided into many different **phyla** (the singular is **phylum**). Your phylum is *Chordata*, and your **subphylum** (a smaller group within a phylum) is *Vertebrata* because you have a backbone.

Each phylum is divided into **classes**. Your class is *Mammalia*. All mammals are warm-blooded and somewhat hairy, with young that feed on the female's milk. Do you still fit?

Each class is divided into **orders**. Your order is *Primata*. All primates have flexible, five-fingered hands and feet. Are you still with me?

Your **family**, the next smaller group, is *Hominidae*. Hominids include all of the two-legged primates. Do you usually walk on two legs? Good, you're correctly classified.

The next subgroup is the **genus**. Your genus is *Homo*—a group that includes both modern and extinct groups of humans.

The **species** is the smallest group. It consists of animals with very similar structures that breed to produce offspring. Modern humans are alone in this species identified as *Homo sapiens*. You're not extinct, so I think you qualify.

Greenpatch Alert:
Endangered and Threatened Species

There are almost 700 animal and plant species listed as threatened or endangered in the U.S. by the federal government (endangered species are worse off than threatened species) and many more worldwide. Endangered or threatened species are listed by the federal government only after they are in severe trouble. Scientists must petition the Secretary of the Interior in Washington, D.C., asking that a species be listed. They must provide information on the decline of the species population and the condition of its habitat. If the petition is accepted, then the species becomes a candidate for listing as threatened or endangered.

Additionally, state governments have their own rules for listing species. Recovery funds are provided for listed species, and their habitats can be classified as "critical" and more readily preserved. Because of a lack of money and because of political debate, thousands of candidates have yet to be listed.

What You Can Do

If you want to know more about federal endangered species, look for the Greenpatch Alerts in this book, and write the Fish and Wildlife Service at the address below. They can send you a list of all endangered and threatened species, facts about the Endangered Species Act, and information about the recovery programs for listed species.

To find out about endangered species that are only listed by your state, write the Fish and Game Department in your state's capital.

You can also write your state senators and state representatives to ask them how you can support the Endangered Species Act and help endangered species in your area. To get their addresses, call the local chapter of the League of Women Voters, your city hall, or your local library.

Write to: Division of Endangered Species, U.S. Fish and Wildlife Service, Arlington Square, 4401 N. Fairfax Drive, Arlington, VA 22203. Send a self-addressed, stamped envelope with your letter so it is easier for a representative to write you back.

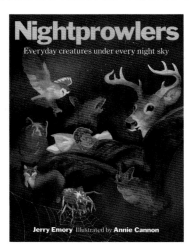

The Greenpatch Kids Want You!

All over the world, this very minute, kids just like you are working to make the earth a safe place for all living things. There is a lot to do. You and your friends can help. If you do, you will be joining hundreds and thousands of kids everywhere. Here are some ways you can get started:

1. Join the Greenpatch Kids.

The Greenpatch Kids is an alliance of young people who want to learn about the environment and how to protect it. Anyone can join. If your copy of this book includes a mail-back card, complete the form with your name and address, and send it in. (Don't forget a stamp.) If there isn't a card in your book, write your name, address, age, and school on a piece of paper, put it in an envelope, and send it to the address below. You will receive a Greenpatch membership card and a free copy of the *Greenpatch News*, which is full of ideas for projects and will tell you what other kids are doing. Write to:

Greenpatch Kids
Harcourt Brace Children's Books
525 B Street, Suite 1900
San Diego, CA 92101

2. Start a Greenpatch Kids group.

Governments and big environmental groups can't always work in your neighborhood, but you and your friends sure can! All you need is an adult sponsor, some friends, and a plan.

Do a neighborhood bio-survey. What animals and plants live there? Are any of them endangered? What can you do to protect them? Start a pollution watch. The health of our earth *starts in your neighborhood*.

3. Tell us about your project.

The people who made this book and Greenpatch Kids everywhere want to know what you are doing. Your idea might be just what someone else needs. If you have a project that works, send us a description. Be sure to include your name, address, age, and telephone number, in case we need to contact you for more information.

4. Contact and work with other groups.

To get help for your project, or to find out what to do in your neighborhood, contact other groups. The largest environmental group for young people is *Kids for Saving Earth*. It costs $7 to join (or $15 for your group), but they will send you a free information pack if you write or call them. Ask them if there is already a KSE group in your town. Write *Kids for Saving Earth*, P.O. Box 47247, Plymouth, MN 55447, or phone 612-525-0002.